Sex, Intimacy & Lying About Love

Also by Thom W. King and Debora Peterson

The Good Girls' Guide to Great Sex

Sex, Intimacy & Lying About Love

5,000 Men Go to Bed and Tell the Truth

Thom W. King

Debora Peterson

Three Rivers Press • New York

Published by Three Rivers Press, a division of Crown Publishers, Inc., 201 East 50th Street, New York, New York 10022. Member of the Crown Publishing Group.

Random House, Inc. New York, Toronto, London, Sydney, Auckland
www.randomhouse.com/

THREE RIVERS PRESS is a trademark of Crown Publishers, Inc.
Printed in the United States of America

Library of Congress Cataloging-in-Publication Data
King, Thom W.
Sex, intimacy, and lying about love : 5,000 men go to bed and tell the truth / by Thom W. King and Debora Peterson. — 1st ed.
1. Men—United States—Sexual behavior. 2. Intimacy (Psychology)—United States. I. Peterson, Debora. II. Title
HQ28.K54 1998
306.7'081—dc21 97-28698

ISBN 0-609-80278-X

10 9 8 7 6 5 4 3 2 1

First Edition

Acknowledgments

To the men between the covers, and you know who you are, I thank you. If someone had told me I would write sex books when I grew up with a crazy man named Thom King, I would have laughed very big. Well, look who's not laughing.

I've had strange jobs in my life, including my short summer driving an ice cream truck with children running out in front of me from all directions waving money and screaming their heads off, but nothing comes close to the past several years in working on these books. Oh, and then there was the job I had working as a 911 dispatcher and the dump truck company I drove for. Still, nothing compares.

The men and women we've met have been exciting, compelling, provocative, funny, and most of all, very real. What a refreshing project! I really appreciate their willingness to talk to us about their most personal thoughts and opinions. Now, if I could just get Thom to quit telling me stories about *his* sex life, I'd have it made.

Many thanks to all the men, good and not-so-good, that participated in our venture. Thom and I had all the fun we could possibly stand while working on this book. I'd like to thank a friend in particular—one of the good guys—Ben

Willingham, for his enthusiasm and moral support of our projects. Ben can't wait to see what we're up to next. Frankly, neither can we.

I'd also like to say I'm so thrilled to be working with the best in the business; our editor Shaye Areheart, associate editor Dina Siciliano, and all the fabulous folks at Three Rivers Press, Crown, and Random House. How I love New York! I'm still wondering what we did to deserve you guys. Many, many thanks.

Everyone should have the pleasure of meeting our literary agent, Meredith Bernstein, a vivacious woman with endless energy and a refreshing passion for her work. Thanks again, Meredith!

Last, but certainly not least, thanks to my family. They love me and put up with me no matter what. I love you deeply.

—D.P.

When I was eight years old I let Sara, a neighborhood girl who was all of nine or ten, talk me into playing show and tell in the garage behind my house.

Right at the moment when I was proudly showing her my erect little "boyhood" we were discovered by my mom. Sara started crying her eyes out while her little flowered panties hung bunched around her ankles in the dirt. Mom came running after me, dropping her wet clothes basket as she ran. She jerked me up by my arm and proceeded to spank the excitement right out of my body. She told Sara to put her clothes back on and go home. She'd call her mother in a few minutes and tell her what we were up to.

I was sent to my room and told to think about what I had

done. I remember thinking that getting caught was worse than seeing Sara's privates. Then Mom added that Dad would give me real punishment when he got off from work.

The one time in his life that Dad came home early from work was on this day. Mom met him at the front door and described in detail my exploratory escapades. She told him to take off his belt and give me a whippin'.

Dad came to my room, shut the door behind him, and held his belt in his hand. He told me to bend over and take my punishment. As I prepared for unbearable horror, I heard a loud *whack*. I felt no pain. Was I numb with fear? Had he severed my nerve endings? I watched in awe as Dad whipped my bedpost three more times.

As he left the room he said, "Son, you have to watch out for those little girls. They will get you into trouble."

I've lived by those words ever since. For this reason, and a million more, I dedicate this book to Thomas T. King, my father. He is currently eighty-four years old, and still giving me wise advice daily.

Interviewing more than 5,000 men about their sexuality has been an interesting job these past two years. Some people sell insurance, some build houses. Debora Peterson and I are lucky enough to make a living asking strangers questions that would cause most people to get slapped—or maybe even arrested. Is this a great world we live in, or what?

Thanks to all the men who answered our rude questions and bared their souls.

A round of applause also goes to our family at Three Rivers Press, Crown Publishers, and Random House, especially Shaye and Dina. We love those big thick packages you send that seem to arrive out of the blue with New York postmarks. Thanks for the support and insight. And finally, to Meredith, our tireless literary agent, keep on making those phone calls and depositing those advances. All you guys do good work! It is an honor to work with you.

—T.W.K.

Author's Note

The issue of safe sex is of prime concern to us. Sex is dangerous today. Though progress is being made daily in fighting HIV and AIDS, the best medicine is prevention.

The stories you are about to read cover thousands of men and decades of experiences. We do not advocate promiscuous sex. Free love is really a thing of the past. Be safe. Love with all your heart, but protect your health and those you love by practicing safe sex. Live to tell the story. We'd love to hear your sexual update twenty years from now.

When a cure for AIDS is found, we'll all party. Until then, be loving, protected, and safe.

Contents

Sex, Intimacy & Lying About Love

Introduction

Sex, Intimacy, and Lying About Love ASKS THOUSANDS OF men, from assorted ages, backgrounds, and experiences, questions about sex, self, love, women, and relationships. The 313 questions found in this book were developed by asking thousands of women the following simple question: If you could ask men anything, what would it be?

Sex, Intimacy, and Lying About Love is the follow-up book to our first effort, *The Good Girls' Guide to Great Sex*. During the three years we spent putting together the first book, we interviewed thousands of women about their lives, opinions, and needs—and they always had questions about men. Many questions. Women kept telling us that we needed to do another book about men. Women were curious about the male animal. They wanted answers. They wanted insight. They wanted a little relief to their constant bewilderment.

So while we were interviewing women, we began to interview men, also. Our second book, the one you now hold in your hands, is *for* men, *by* men, and *about* men, but it is also for the women of the world—the mothers, daughters, wives, and lovers of men across the land—who demanded that we find answers to the questions they most wanted to know. Secretaries, nurses, teachers, housewives—they all helped us develop the best and most revealing questions, the things a woman would like straight, informative answers to. So these questions represent what Good Girls across the spectrum want to know.

This book is the result of thousands of up-close and personal interviews, surveys, and chat sessions. We asked these questions at bars, offices, sporting events, in living rooms, and various other locations. We used whatever tools were necessary to get the information we needed: from E-mail, scanners, modems, snail-mail, faxes, and telephones, to handwritten notes on napkins, beer coasters, shirtsleeves, and hamburger wrappers. It was high-tech one minute, and plain old-fashioned no-tech the next. We talked to guys in groups, solo, and through the mail. Sometimes we would do intense one-on-one interviews with tape recorders. Other times men would hear about our project and get a group of poker buddies together for an all-night talk session. Coworkers photocopied our questions and sent them to regional offices. Brothers sent copies of the questions to siblings across the nation. Friends told friends, strangers compared notes, and a general mass of male opinion began to grow. We called it the snowball that became an avalanche.

Word got out about our venture through almost every means possible, and once men became comfortable with the idea of talking about sex and women, we had a hard time shutting them up. It was a powerful force of thoughts, emotions, and pent-up frustrations.

The answers were surprising, bold, inspiring, outrageous, and sometimes, controversial. Some clichés were personified. Jocks sometimes gave the kind of answers you'd expect them to give. Some lawyers and psychiatrists reflected their backgrounds many times in carefully detailed answers. Blue-collar guys often gave beer-induced answers, and accountants tended to give statistics and support their views with charts and numbers. Then there were those guys who surprised us, and then surprised us yet again. We saw grown men cry about childhood memories of love lost. We heard groups of baseball players wax poetic about the most romantic moments of their lives. We read stories of joy, pain, lust, adventure, and plain old fun.

Men from every background imaginable told us stories of passion. They told us about dreams, needs, desires. Some guys spilled their guts and cried in their whiskey. Some men told of intimate expectations and missed opportunities.

Then some guys were just plain jerks, and proud of it. They bragged about their mean deeds, their thoughtless actions, and their cruel jokes. They were pigs and happy in their filth. They talked of their tricks, lies, and games. They proudly proclaimed their abilities in destroying women's lives. They could name the times and places they had most hurt women in their past. Their sadistic pleasures were sometimes so unmistakable, it hurt to hear their voices.

We interviewed all kinds of people. The answers were candid, and sometimes scary. You never knew what someone was going to say. A meek little guy would become a bragging bore by the middle of the survey. A big, brawny outdoorsman would smile with a sweet sense of pleasure while remembering his high school prom. The examples are endless.

We did discover one major difference between interviewing women and men. For the most part women were comfortable and thoughtful in answering intimate and probing questions about their relationships and sexuality. They would breeze through the questions and had little problem coming up with their answers. Men were entirely different. As much as they may brag about their sexual experiences, when it came right down to putting their thoughts out for the world to see, a lot of men were really shy boys.

We'd watch them struggle with questions, amazed at the range of emotions they would go through to come up with their answers. Some guys would turn beet red. Some would laugh out loud. Nervous giggles would often fill the room. In nearly every group session, one guy would always yell out, "You guys won't believe question ten!"

It seemed that for the most part, men had never really given voice to their sexuality, to what it means to be a man. Women had clearly thought about what they liked, needed, and wanted, but men hadn't verbalized such emotions even to themselves, much less anyone else.

Now they would brag. They would strut. And it was painfully obvious that many had never even considered their sensitive, so-called feminine side. They had amazing difficulty putting into words their thoughts and emotions. The idea of sharing their intimate desires with a group of men was horrifying to many.

As in the first book, we promised complete confidentiality to all those who answered our questions. We wanted the truth. We wanted candid answers. We didn't want men to hold back on their true feelings for fear of discovery. Whereas women appreciated our willingness to be discreet and protect their identities, men *demanded* it. They simply did not want their coworkers to know that they liked being tickled and being cuddled to sleep each night. They seemed to feel that their reputations would be ruined if the rest of the guys knew that their secret desire was to spend a romantic evening in a hot tub with their lover.

So we faced the peculiar phenomenon of having a hulking lumberjack of a man stand in our face and demand that we never tell anyone he likes to read poetry to his wife on the phone. It was touching, but a little sad.

It was apparent that most men had never taken the time to look at the true emotions behind their sex lives. We had hundreds and hundreds of men thank us for letting them be involved in our research. The questions had led them down a personal path of discovery that many had never considered possible. It was a great feeling watching some of these men discover deep emotional feelings that had been buried for years. It was a lot of fun seeing them warm up to the ideas presented.

By the time most men had finished our 313 questions, they were excited about the new possibilities facing them. Some guys seemed invigorated. Some were unambiguously aroused. Some were extremely glad that we didn't use a chalkboard or require them to go answer questions in front of a group. Most of them had writer's cramp, and many of them were heading straight home to their lover for "additional research."

We hope you enjoy reading the results of our efforts. Take advantage of the experience of others. Play and feel, experiment and probe. If Joe enjoyed it, and his lover Jill almost passed out from the intense pleasure, maybe you can start adding it to your sexual menu every now and then. Mostly, we hope you ascertain for your own pleasure what "it" really is. We highly encourage you to take the survey and share it with your lover and friends. There are no right or wrong answers.

You can't flunk this survey. Have fun with it. Let your emotions, memories, and desires come alive and run rampant.

Enjoy your own survey of sharing and learning, at home. Write long answers. Write short quips. Be frank. Be candid. Be outrageous, funny, sad, thoughtful, insightful, sexy, and most of all, *be yourself.*

Although this book is finished, we hope to continue the series with more women, more men, more fun. If you would like to share your answered survey with us, please send us a copy or a cassette copy (if your survey was done orally) in care of:

THE GOOD GIRLS
P.O. Box 50214
Belle Meade Station
Nashville, TN 37205

We continue to believe that sexual knowledge may be the *ultimate* power.

1 Preferences

1. ***Describe great sex.***
2. ***Describe bad sex.***
3. ***What is your favorite time to make love?***
4. ***How long should intercourse last?***
5. ***Do you have sex with the lights on or off? Candles?***
6. ***What music do you like to hear during lovemaking, if any?***
7. ***Do you like to wear cologne? Favorite?***
8. ***Do you like your partner to wear perfume? Favorite?***
9. ***What drives you wild?***
10. ***What drives you away?***
11. ***Describe the perfect woman.***
12. ***Describe the perfect date.***

1. Describe great sex.

Great sex is when I have completely worn my girlfriend down to a puddle of sighs. My balls ache, I'm out of breath and red in the face. My baby is rubbed raw, lying flat on her back, and completely blissed out.

John, 26, carpenter

Great sex is when I have a complete feeling of numbness in my penis after climaxing six times.

Larry, 34, salesperson

Great sex is when I can keep my eyes open and really look at the girl I'm having sex with. The best sex is when I don't have to fantasize that I'm with a supermodel. I usually run away to my private little imaginary world when I have sex and use the girl as a sperm receptacle.

Jerry, 20, student

Great sex is when I have made my lady come until she and I are both empty and no longer have control of our senses. We are both just mush—body, soul, and mind.

Brad, 37, editor

Now, let's see . . . *great* is a huge word in the English language. I don't know if *great* is the appropriate word. Stuck to the ceiling comes to mind when thinking about spectacular sex. When I experience sex that has lifted me to an out-of-body experience, then that's the woman I stay with and continue, as now, to stay with.

Martin, 43, stockbroker

2. Describe bad sex.

Bad sex is when my girlfriend has multiple climaxes and all I get is blue balls.

Mark, 19, student

Bad sex is when I'm having sex simply because my girlfriend

wants me to, instead of having an inner desire of my own. It feels too much like work or duty.

Bob, 43, lawyer

Bad sex is when my girlfriend starts without me and comes all over the sheets just when I get ready to get in bed. She is all tingled out, and I have a boner and a spit-filled fist. Major frustration.

Andy, 24, electrician

Bad sex is when I am too tired to get it up and my girlfriend keeps on trying to get me hard, while all I want to do is turn over and catch some z's. She doesn't seem to understand that even if I'm not in the mood, all she has to do is touch my pecker softly, and since it has a mind of its own, it will still get erect. But, she keeps trying the wrong things and I'm just not in the mood to do anything about it. I really don't mean to hurt her feelings, I just want her to leave me alone.

Tim, 25, auto mechanic

She can be a knockout gorgeous babe with long, slender legs that go up to "there," have big eyes that seem to say, "Come hither, sweet wonderful man," but if she doesn't smell fresh and squeaky-clean, I'm completely turned off and disgusted. Cleanliness is next to godliness.

Gregory, 29, furniture manufacturer

3. What is your favorite time to make love?

When my wife least expects it. I like to do it when she is getting ready for work, or grading papers from her school class.

I like to sneak up on her and ambush her with love, attention, and a hungry tongue.

Jeremy, 30, merchant

My favorite time for sex is when I'm a little drunk and very horny. It could be midnight, it could be noon. Whenever the combination is right, so is the timing. My biological clock is much more important than my Timex.

Sam, 24, housepainter

Anytime I think about sex, I get a boner. So if I am thinking, it is time for sex. If I'm breathing, it is time for sex. That's like asking when is my favorite time to be alive. The answer is "all the time."

Alex, 19, cowhand

My favorite time to make love is when we both have plenty of time and can fill each other's senses completely, until we can no longer stand it and end up fucking our brains out. Now, just plain ole sex, well, that's a different story altogether.

William, 43, toolmaker

When she least expects me to slither up from behind her and "take her" to heavenly places.

Ben, 24, accountant

4. How long should intercourse last?

It should last until neither of us can do any more than moan, or maybe groan.

Andy, 36, baker

Sex should last until we get our fill. My mother taught me to always clean my plate. My scoutmaster taught me to finish what I started. So when it comes to good loving, I firmly believe that as long as I have an erection, I must keep on moving, pumping, and coming.

Ronald, 29, forest ranger

Sex should last until my balls go flat and ache.

Trey, 34, delivery route driver

There is no time limit on intercourse. It can be from a fantastic two-minute quickie to a six-hour marathon—as long as both people are truly satisfied, it is long enough.

Frank, 39, engineer

I can't rest until I know in my heart that she is full of me and satisfied that I have done for her what no other man could do. If I can't accomplish that, make her feel better than any other man can, then I don't deserve her.

Jonathan, 32, bakery store owner

5. Do you have sex with the lights on or off? Candles?

When I was in college, I dated a girl who loved to fill a room with lit candles and make love. Most of the time it was fine with me, but once after a particularly lengthy session of sex, wine, and music, we awoke to a room full of thick, smelly smoke. The candle on the night table had burned down and actually set my plastic eyeglasses on fire. The frame was in flames, one lens was completely gone, and the other one was a molten puddle. It cost me over two hundred dollars to replace them.

Scott, 29, computer programmer

When I was young, I loved to see the faces of the women I made love to. Now after thirty years of marriages, affairs, divorces, and a bitter dose of reality, I'd rather turn the lights completely off. I'm tired of seeing the hurt, bitterness, and impossible expectations on the faces of the women I bed these days.

Joe, 53, business manager

I like to get her in a totally dark room and play with her with my tongue, fingers, and legs. I like to roam and taste and probe every part of my baby. Sometimes I end up in places I wouldn't normally go, and that is part of the fun. I love to surprise my girlfriend, and when you french-kiss her nose in total darkness, it does tend to get her attention.

Bobby, 20, construction worker

Whether the lights are on or off really doesn't matter to me. As long as we are both in the mood for some good lovin', there could be a spotlight on us and I wouldn't care. Sometimes my girl wants all the romantic things like candles, flowers, wine, you know, and that gets me just as hot as simply watching her undressing for bed. I believe it's all in your frame of mind.

Adam, 29, manager

I used to like making love with the lights on until one night I saw my girlfriend bleed. It was the most frightening thing I've ever seen. We were going at it with everything we had in us. We had done the oral pleasures already, and I was drilling her just the way she likes, hard and pounding, my butt pushing with all I am worth, zapping my strength and pushing us both to a climax and a deep sigh. Then it happened. I rolled over to get up on my knees and lean over her limp body to kiss her romantically in the bliss of our afterglow, when my eyes glanced across her legs and the bed. Bright red blood was literally everywhere. I fainted and fell from the bed and onto the floor, hitting my head on the corner of the night table. The lamp fell and broke into several pieces—my head was bleeding all over the floor and I was out cold. Lisa had to get up and call 911. The paramedics came and took me away. Of course Lisa went with me to the hospital and eventually everything was fine. I just had a nasty bump on my head for about a week—and nightmares.

Tony, 27, marketing specialist

6. What music do you like to hear during lovemaking, if any?

I am a rock-and-roller. Loud, hard rock is the only music allowed in my bedroom. I don't want something I can dance to. I want something that helps me fuck my girlfriend's butt off. I don't want sensitive love songs, pretty poems, or whining wimp sounds. I want the bass to knock me in the nuts and make the posters on my wall shake.

Joshua, 20, college student

When my wife whispers in my ear that she loves me with all her heart, that is total music to my ears. It has been true for over fifty years.

Sam, 68, retired steelworker

I like sweet soul music from the sixties and seventies. Not rap. Not gangster stuff. Not even disco. I like Al Green, Isaac

Hayes, Barry White, classic Motown. I like music you can slow-grind to, drink wine and make sweet love with. The irony of this is that I am probably the whitest, palest, least soulful guy you will ever meet. I run numbers all day as a CPA, and if you wanted to create a definition of "white bread" you'd find me staring back at you. Maybe the contrast is what I like. Or maybe I just like the songs and can sing along with every one of thousands.

Stan, 45, accountant

I like to listen to the sounds of jazz or Latin music. As its rhythm increases in tempo so does my thrusting in and out.

Carl, 23, sales representative

I'm an alternative kind of guy. Tori Amos makes my balls hard and my palms sweat. That's the right thing for me, love it, love it, makes me want to do it, do it. My girlfriend wonders if I ever got near Tori, would I ask her out. I don't think she has anything to seriously worry over.

Rob, 26, fast-food worker

7. Do you like to wear cologne? Favorite?

I like to wear women's perfume. I always have. It may have started when I was little and went shopping with my mom. I always played with the pretty sampler bottles at the cosmetics counter while Mom was picking out lipstick. I'd always leave the store smelling like a cheap whore, or an overly scented grandmother. I'm still up to my old tricks. You can always tell when I'm coming by just taking a big breath.

Tim, 33, entertainer

My wife loves my natural sweat. She loves to smell my T-shirts and underwear. I used to wear the typical shaving lotions, but she always said they made her sneeze. She gave me such a hard time about covering up my natural smell that I finally just stopped using anything. I work outside and sweat all day long. At night I put my dirty clothes in the basket by the washer. She will let them stay there for a week or more and then drown herself in the aroma. At first I thought it was a little weird, but after three years of marriage, and a totally wonderful sex life, I'm not complaining.

Mark, 28, computer programmer

I wear cologne all the time, but the scent I love most is the earthy smell of a woman. Since they don't bottle that, I am not particular about the cologne I wear.

John, 46, real estate

No. I like the smell of a woman's body. The natural lusty smell of sex, cum, and sweat. There's no manufacturer of that kind of aroma. It can't be bought.

Pat, 22, carpenter

8. Do you like your partner to wear perfume? Favorite?

I like to smell the musk of arousal on my partner's panties. Often while I'm working on the computer at night, she'll put on her red teddy and walk through the den, with a glass of red wine and a moist crotch. The natural sexuality which fills my nostrils is overpowering. I usually lose whatever file I'm working on in my haste to shut the computer off and get to the bedroom.

Daryl, 28, accountant

I love to buy my girlfriend nice perfume. She collects the bottles and always gives me a special sexual treat when I add to her collection. I once bought her a sample collection of ten French perfumes in little miniature bottles, and we spent a week putting those essential oils in some very sensual places. I still catch the little whiff of a scent when I rub my chest hair.

Randy, 33, regional sales director

I like for my lady friend to wear cologne, but not so much that her smell stays around for hours after she has left. Some women wear such strong stuff that it overpowers my senses. How could it possibly turn any man on when he can't breathe without choking on the smell.

Mark, 33, express-delivery driver

Obsession is justifiably named. When my Isabella wears it to bed, I'm an animal.

Barry, 25, gardening supply store

9. What drives you wild?

I like an aggressive woman who knows what she wants. I don't always want to be the aggressor. Sometimes I just like to be seduced and fucked hard.

Jessie, 42, bartender

I love it when my girlfriend puts her tongue in my ear. We can be in the middle of the mall shopping, and one flick from her wicked little tongue will have me hiding an erection and looking for a bench to sit down on.

Barney, 23, telemarketer

I love it when my girlfriend puts her finger in her wet vagina, and then brings her juicy finger to my lips. I go insane and become rock hard. She does it while we are driving. She does it while we are waiting in line to see a movie. She does it pretty much anywhere and anytime she wants to, and it always drives me wild. I love the taste, and I love the total nastiness of her actions. It brings out the animal in me.

Donald, 37, stockbroker

A simple come-hither look from the right person can drive me wild. I guess I'm just a young, horny college boy that does not get enough sex.

Collin, 19, student

Garters. High heels, silk stockings, and a lacy garter puts me over the top and lands me on the roof. Good thing I don't get nosebleeds. My sweetheart owns lots and lots of garters.

Kevin, 26, highway department

10. What drives you away?

A woman who wants to own me because we have sex once. Just because I might want a little taste of her doesn't mean that she is all I want to eat the rest of my life.

Will, 18, waiter

A woman who is so busy worrying about whether I'm happy while we are making love that she can't relax and enjoy it herself. I don't want her to be so focused on me that she ignores herself. It just puts pressure on me, and I don't need any more pressure.

George, 42, investor

A woman whose middle name is "Mommy."

Brad, 25, photographer

Recently divorced women with kids used to be my favorite conquest, but it became too easy. They are so needy and willing to compromise, it takes all the fun out of the romance. They see a new man as the answer to all their sexual, financial, and family problems. Instant lover, Daddy, and moneybags. So when I see a minivan in the driveway and a kid's soccer outfit hanging on the clothesline, I know the sex would be easy, but the excess baggage would be far too heavy.

Anthony, 40, physician

A woman who wants to dominate everything in my life, who wants to be a part of everything I do. I can't even take a pee without her wanting to know where I'm going.

Daryl, 34, policeman

Selfishness can turn me off and send me running out the door instantly. It is unforgivable and disgusting. I met this beautiful woman at a cocktail party fund-raiser and asked her out to dinner the following week. She accepted and I was thrilled. It took all of about forty-five minutes into the date for me to see the selfishness she possessed. I couldn't wait to get home. My penis was more limp than the spaghetti on my plate. In fact, I think my pecker didn't act right for about a month I was so turned off.

Todd, 32, party supply store owner

11. Describe the perfect woman.

Pointy tits, tight vagina, no teeth, and chronic laryngitis. And it would be great if she was eighteen and blond.

Phil, 20, student

The perfect woman doesn't exist. Perfection is an unobtainable goal in a human, male or female.

Abe, 21, counselor

The perfect woman always laughs at my jokes, supports me in times of need, and loves me with a passion undying. She shares my dreams, enthusiasms, hopes, and desires. She is short, tall, red hair, blond, twenty, forty, rich or poor. She could be anyone and live anywhere. I will probably spend the rest of my life looking for her.

Nick, 37, dentist

I know it sounds corny, but the perfect woman would be just like my mom. And I don't mean that in any sick way. Mom always loved me unconditionally. She fed my body and my mind. And she wouldn't let me get away with any bullshit. I'm looking for a little bit of my mom in every woman I go out with.

Sam, 34, computer technician

My perfect woman is a twenty-year-old virgin, with a million-dollar trust fund, no driver's license, and the ability to crack walnuts with her thighs.

Jack, 40, insurance executive

Since I do not believe that there is a perfect woman or man, I guess I would like for my true love to have a sharp mind, good looks, drive me wild in bed, but be her own person and have a life outside of mine. My ideal woman knows who she is and what she wants out of life and is not afraid to fight for it. That's not too much to ask for, is it? By the way, I'm still looking for her.

Robert, 36, store owner

Faithful. Women who cheat are even more disgusting than men who cheat. I'd like to take both sexes, people who cheat, and throw them all in a state—maybe Wyoming with the tumbleweeds—and make them live with each other. The more I think about it, the better I like that idea. Confine them together, they deserve each other.

Tracy, 30, office supply store worker

12. Describe the perfect date.

The perfect date is one where we don't really do anything but be together. I know it sounds corny, but a day in the park, a shared pizza, and a night of loving sex is really my idea of perfection. Spending money I don't have on meals that I don't like in exotic cities on vacation isn't nearly as satisfying as a low-cost local day in the sunshine and sack.

Bo, 27, manager trainee

Where I don't have to be polite, charming, interesting, or funny. I just come over to her house, walk in the door, and attack her warm, wet, willing body. I devour her passion. I drink her juices. I pound her insides into a frothy milk shake of sex and sweat. I make love till I pass out. That is my idea of a perfect date, and as you well know, I have never had a perfect date in my entire life. I probably never will have one.

Van, 24, baker

My idea of a perfect date is one where everything goes smoothly from the time I pick her up to the time the date is over and I look forward to seeing her again the next day.

Kirk, 26, limousine driver

A *Playboy* magazine, a bag of chips and dip, a six-pack of beer, and my hand. I just broke up with my wife, I'm being sued for divorce and alimony, and I'm not in a good mood.

Robert, 31, hardware store worker

2 First Sexual Experiences

1. ***Who told you about sex?***
2. ***How did you react when you learned about sex?***
3. ***Who taught you about sex?***
4. ***Describe your first sexual feelings. How old were you?***
5. ***When did you lose your virginity (have intercourse fully)? Describe the experience.***
6. ***Did your first sexual experience live up to your expectations?***
7. ***Whom did you tell, if anyone, about your first experience with intercourse?***

1. Who told you about sex?

My older sister told me about the birds and bees when she was twelve and I was nine. I called her a big fat liar and went crying to Mommy. When Momma gave her a spanking, I figured she must have told me a really big lie. It was about five years before I realized her spanking was for telling me the truth.

Jeff, 33, physical therapist

My cousin Ralphie told our neighborhood gang about sex when we were eight. We knew he was probably right, but the thought of our parents doing it that way was very, very upsetting. We figured there was one way for sluts, tramps, and bad people; and another, totally dignified and respectful method for people we knew, like our parents. We were wrong. We actually caught Ralphie's parents banging their brains out one Friday night, and it was anything but dignified.

George, 37, industrial designer

My baby-sitter, Mary, was fifteen and I was eleven. She told me about the birds and the bees. Then she had me put my hand under her dress and feel her. It was the most powerful moment of my life. I was scared, confused, and so excited I thought I would pass out. I can still smell her musky scent twenty years later. I never had sex with her or anyone else until I was eighteen, but I spent every day between my first touch and my first intercourse thinking about it.

Norm, 33, driving instructor

I learned about sex the old-fashioned way, the streets. My mother was a single parent and I guess she was too busy to tell me about the facts of life. I don't blame her, she probably figured that since I was a boy, I wouldn't listen to her anyway. She was right.

Bart, 24, clerk

My baby-sitter. I thought she was lying, just trying to scare me or something. Little did I know she was telling the awful truth. She started with oral sex, describing this tongue-licking, slurping stuff, and I couldn't imagine that for the life of me. *"Put my mouth on what?"* I cried. I really thought she was crazy. In fact, I got her fired. I told Mom and Dad I saw her doing drugs in the living room. She still lives down the street and I see her from time to time, but she never speaks to me. I feel bad about it now, but I can't blame her for being mad at me. I should thank her for the information, but at ten years old, she scared the crap right out of me.

Charley, 25, telemarketing manager

2. How did you react when you learned about sex?

I turned a thousand shades of red. I was ten and my mother decided it was time for me to know the facts. I would much rather have waited about a dozen years or more. My father tried to tell me, but he was going so slow and having such a hard time with the subject matter that Mom finally just told me herself. I remember being embarrassed for Dad and myself. It was a bad precedent. Women have been telling me about sex ever since.

Dan, 32, illustrator

I really, really liked the idea. It seemed natural. It seemed logical. And it finally made sense why my penis became hard as a rock and stuck straight out when I'd see up a girl's dress on the playground at recess. I didn't feel like such a freak anymore.

Jack, 58, security specialist

When I found out about sex, I was in the front seat of a Pontiac. Fumbling around with my girl, acting like I knew exactly what I was doing, when all along I was scared to death. I was afraid that I was not doing it right and would not live up to her expectations. I was wrong, she was as scared as I was and it was all over in probably ten minutes flat. What a lesson!

Bobby, 25, stockman

I had been reading *Playboy* magazines and couldn't wait to try some of this stuff on a girl. Man, was I dumb and dumbest. My first stab at making out with a girl was about as successful as a train wreck. She couldn't wait to get away from me and, frankly, neither could I. I would tell my son not to believe, or try, everything you read in a girlie magazine.

Vernon, 67, retired salesman

3. Who taught you about sex?

My eleven-year-old next-door neighbor told me about sex and showed me how our parts were different. I was ten, and she loved to play with my little boner. Unfortunately, in looking back, I now realize that she really was playing mind games. She liked to kiss me, grab my penis through my pants, and then get me excited. She would make me pull down my pants and show her my erection. Then she would hit it with her hand and sometimes even try to kick it. She would tell me to make my erection go away and make fun of my little pecker. It was humiliating, but very exciting. She moved away the following year. I often wonder what happened to her. I hope she is still fascinated by erections and making men hard.

Tracy, 33, druggist

I learned about sex from an ancient "marriage manual" I found hidden in the attic. It had line drawings, and big words, but I was able to figure out what part went where. I used this little bit of knowledge to convince my next-door neighbor to let me touch her little twelve-year-old pussy. That little girl is now my wife, and we have three kids, a dog, and a station wagon. What we don't have is a marriage manual hidden in the attic. Our biggest worry is keeping the kids off the sex lines of the Internet.

Bernie, 39, business owner

I am a self-taught man; I kept on trying until I got it right. Besides, "practice makes perfect."

Tom, 34, instructor

My first experience with lovemaking was wonderful. I was eighteen and just out of high school. She was woman of thirty-nine, so I lay there, watched intently, and learned. A lot. This woman worked at the same place I did and asked me out. I couldn't believe it and I couldn't wait to go. We had a candlelight dinner for two at a tiny Italian restaurant with wine and the works. Then a moonlight drive through Central Park in a horse-drawn carriage. By the time we arrived at her apartment, I was so nervous and excited, I couldn't wait for the lessons to begin. Now that I think back on it, it was the best sex I ever had and still is. I would have married her if there weren't laws against having two husbands.

Steven, 30, counselor

4. Describe your first sexual feelings. How old were you?

I was twelve years old and found an old *Playboy* magazine in a cardboard box down by the creek. I didn't care about reading any of the stories, but I will always remember the photos of the girls of Texas. There were wonderful pages filled with bare breasted Southern girls playing in the great outdoors. I fell totally in lust with an incredible blond babe with perfect firm breasts, totally edible nipples, and a set of legs that looked as if she could crack walnuts with them. She was riding bareback on a horse, nude, and I spent many childhood nights wishing I could have been her own little stud pony. I probably had erections before I found these pictures, but my first erections of desire were caused by her image. I have subconsciously spent my life trying to find this woman of my dreams.

Joel, 33, scriptwriter

My first sexual feelings came about when I was eleven years old. I was in church listening to the preacher go on and on about hell and fire and eternal damnation. It was the typical sermon designed to scare you into being good, because hell was so bad. One of the women in the pew beside us had on a blouse with a button open. She didn't know it, but from my viewpoint I could see all of her breast. I saw her heaving chest and her big brown nipple, and it made my penis explode. I instantly came in my pants and hid the spot on my best Sunday trousers with the hymn book. I'd love to say the book was opened to "Rock of Ages," but that would be too ironic.

Jeff, 34, financial planner

I was around thirteen and my neighbor down the street had on a real short skirt and was not too shy about the way she sat down on her sofa. She did not have on any panties, and I got an immediate erection. I was so scared and embarrassed that I ran all the way home and up to my bedroom. I actually hid under my bed. I thought something was wrong with me. In looking back, I believe she knew exactly what she was doing and was enjoying every minute of my embarrassment. Boy, did I grow up quick.

Teddy, 23, military

5. When did you lose your virginity (have intercourse fully)? Describe the experience.

I was sixteen and on summer vacation in Detroit. My cousin set me up on a date with his girlfriend's best friend, Jackie. She was a city girl with long black hair, developing breasts, and the softest thighs I can ever remember. I was her "country" boyfriend and she loved my Southern accent. She would take me to meet her friends and tell me to say *ya'll* all the time. In the two months I spent with her, I went from experiencing my first French kiss, to feeling my first breast, to touching my first vagina, to getting a hand job. The final week of the summer, she took me down into the basement of her home, pulled out the roll-up bed, took off all her clothes, and pulled me on top of her. My heart was racing. I was burning up with passion and excitement. She directed me into her soaking vagina and started my virgin rhythm. After about six hours of imagined ecstasy and probably five minutes of real time, I climaxed deeply and emotionally inside her. We smothered each other with kisses and pledges of undying love. We were pen pals for about six months afterwards. I heard that she married a sailor at seventeen and dropped out of school. I still have fond memories of my city girl and her big-city ways.

Charles, 35, schoolteacher

I lost my virginity on my eighteenth birthday at a whorehouse in Memphis. The woman was ugly, saggy, and smelled like piss. I fucked her like she was Miss America. I came in about five minutes and didn't want to pull out of her. I tried to kiss her and she screamed for the bouncer. It was probably the worst sex I ever had or ever gave, but I remember it more than most of the sex I've had with my wife in the past thirty-five years.

George, 62, manufacturer

I was fifteen, and raised in the country. I was out in the field cutting hay on a hot summer afternoon when I decided to take a break and go for a swim to cool off a bit. As I walked over to a pond that was on our property, I saw this girl who lived close by on our road and had been trying to catch my attention for weeks swimming in our pond totally nude. I saw her as I was approaching the water, though she still had not seen me. I slipped out of my clothes and waded very quietly into the water. As she turned around, I reached for her and playfully pulled her under. She gasped for air and then realized who had her. Needless to say we started playing around and one thing led to another. After about twenty minutes of playing in the water, we made our way up to the bank where we had the most amazing sex as the sun was setting for the evening. I never did finish getting the hay in that day.

Billy, 27, farmer

My first time with sex was the night of my senior prom. My date's father was a dentist and she took me to his office after our night of dancing, dinner, and stupid awards. We had been dating for two years and we were going off to different colleges. She seemed to be on a mission to lose her virginity before the end of our senior year. I now know that she had been planning her big night for weeks. I'm not sure if she had a bet with her best friend over who was going to lose her hymen first, or if her biological clock was just ticking way too loudly. All I know for certain is that she had decided to take me along for the ride. It was a great trip.

We drove up to her father's clinic around two in the morning. She had taken the extra key from her father's desk in the den. She had already put candles in the waiting room. She had a bottle of Communion wine chilled on the floor next to two glasses. A blanket was spread out and two silk pillows were nearby. Judy must certainly have read her share of romance novels, because she had perfectly orchestrated the entire moment. While she lit the candles, I opened the wine. We toasted to love and gulped down our glasses. She told me she had had a perfect prom, and that she wanted to end it on a perfect note. She said the night was historic and that she was glad I was going to be the person to make her a real woman.

She kissed me and told me to unzip her prom dress. With shaky fingers I pulled the zipper down, and her gown fell to the floor. She was completely nude and shaking in the candlelight. I loved her with all my heart and all my energy. What we didn't have in experience, we made up for in enthusiasm. There was a great pleasure in knowing that we were both virgins. We really took each other on an adventure. She had been on the pill all through high school. Her mother told her she needed them to make her periods come regularly. We both knew it was to make her periods come, period. So when I had my first climax in a woman, I didn't have to pull out and spill my seed—I just plunged deeper into her, looked straight in her eyes, and rammed my tongue down her throat.

We held each other until the sun came up. Before we left, she took me to her father's dentist chair. She turned on the laughing gas and we shared the mask for a few minutes. It was a great way to end the night: ex-virgins, drunk on wine, laughing our heads off. We made it back to her parents' house just as the other kids in the neighborhood were coming home from their postprom breakfast.

After twenty years, I still have a love-hate relationship with dentists. I hate the pain, but I love the memories.

Willie, 40, reporter

My first time was on my wedding night at age twenty-five. I was raised in a religious household. I went to church Sunday mornings, Sunday nights, and Wednesday nights. I was told to wait till marriage for sex, and I did. I met my wife at a Bible college and we dated for three years and married our senior year. I am the proud father of two teenage girls, and I still love my wife deeply. We have a wonderful sex life. We make passionate love two or three times a week. We are loving, frisky, and adventurous. We take care of each other's needs both spiritually and sexually. Just because we preach the word of God doesn't mean we can't have a fantastic sex life. We make love to the glory of God and rejoice in the pleasure it gives us.

Harry, 45, minister

I don't like to recall my first time. It was awful and gangly. I fumbled so much that I was sure I would not stay hard enough to be able to do anything. It was over in just a few short strokes. I'm glad my girl didn't give up on me after that fiasco. We dated throughout high school and were married a year after we graduated. We are still married today, and I can honestly say that we have a fantastic sex life. I think the best part of it was the fact that we learned about sex together. I like to think that we grew up with each other.

Terry, 30, pharmacist

6. Did your first sexual experience live up to your expectations?

I liked my first climax so much, I lost interest in sports, camping, cars, and nearly everything else. I have been chasing women ever since and am basically always trying to recapture that first time. It doesn't work, but I have a hell of a time trying.

James, 27, hairstylist

I'm a guy. What do you think? I was born to fuck.

Steve, 23, road worker

In a word, *yes!* It was beyond my wildest expectations. It was greeeat! Actually, I think it was so very good because I didn't know what to expect.

Tim, 24, salesclerk

7. Whom did you tell, if anyone, about your first experience with intercourse?

I had been lying about it for two years before I actually had sex, so by the time it really happened, it was too late to tell anybody. And my lies were so much better than the reality that there didn't seem to be much of a point to telling anyway.

Steve, 27, mechanic

I told my best friend because we had a bet about who would lose it first. I thought I won, but I later found out that Jerry had taken my sister's cherry a month before I got my first piece from his cousin Cheryl. He didn't tell me because he thought I would have killed him. He was right.

Chuck, 45, trucker

I am the quiet type so I don't kiss and tell. I cherish the memories and the girl that I lost my virginity to. Some things are not to be bragged about and I respect the fact that she didn't tell anyone either. I believe that's part of what made it so special.

Bailey, 29, account manager

3 Your Sexual Profile

1. ***How many sexual partners have you had?***
2. ***How often do you have sex?***
3. ***How important is sex in your life?***
4. ***Are you happy with your sex life?***
5. ***What makes your sex life better than other people's?***
6. ***If you could change anything about your sex life, what would it be?***
7. ***Who do you think has a better sex life than you, and why?***
8. ***What is your special talent that makes you wonderful in bed?***
9. ***What do you wish you were better at doing sexually?***
10. ***What's the first thing you notice when you meet a woman?***
11. ***Have you ever had any problems with sexual performance? If so, how did you handle them?***
12. ***Are you sexually attracted to women much younger than yourself? If so, why?***
13. ***How do you relate to much younger women?***

14. What do you think motivates men to date women twenty or so years younger than themselves? Is it mostly a sexual or physical attraction?

1. How many sexual partners have you had?

I've had two. I've had sex with about ten women, but I only care to remember two of them as partners. And what is even more pathetic is that neither of the two include my three ex-wives.

Andy, 54, grocer

Before AIDS, I prided myself on my list of lovers. Now remembering how I exposed myself to disease chills me to the bone. My love list has potentially become my death list.

Jackie, 35, city planner

I lost count after thirty. It used to really matter. I felt like I was in a race or something to screw as many women as possible. But somewhere along the way I lost interest. I doubt if I could tell you the last ten women I've slept with. I'd rather watch a good basketball game and drink beer than put myself through all the hassle of trying to find some new skirt to chase. I've become boring, I guess.

Nelson, 32, retailer

I do not kiss and count, I've had as many partners as I've wanted to have. I have been practicing safe sex since I first started and still practice it today. I do not brag about my conquests.

Mack, 28, truck driver

2. How often do you have sex?

I try to have sex daily. I'm pretty high energy, and climaxing is my favorite way to go to sleep. If my girlfriend isn't in the mood, my fist is always willing and able.

Ernie, 20, prelaw student

I'm gay, and I have sex every time my lover says, "Now." I'd probably be just as horny if I were born straight, but the fact is that I simply love the feel of ejaculation. It is my drug, my vice, my passion. Without my climaxes, I am a mere shell of a man.

Joseph, 26, telemarketer

I know that the feeling of climaxing evolved in order to preserve the species. Face it, if it hurt to cum, no one would do it. But since it feels so good, guys want to come all the time. In the survival-of-the-species plan, a guy cums in as many women as possible to make as many babies as possible. Now with society and technology, the need to reproduce is lessened. But I, for one, still feel the need to share my sperm with as many warm vaginas as possible. I consider it my personal quest.

William, 24, graduate student

If I don't have some type of sex every day, I turn into this SOB that no one wants to be around. Luckily my girl has a very healthy sexual drive and we always take care of one another's needs and desires.

Jimmy, 35, chef

3. How important is sex in your life?

Sex is the reason I'm polite, generous, and attentive. If I stop being these things, my girlfriend cuts off my sex life. So I guess you could say that sex made me the person I am today: a phony, weak-kneed yes-man who is too spineless to say what he really means.

Neil, 32, real estate agent

I read a book once that said I would be rich and successful if I could transfer my sex drive into a love of money. Well, I'm still poor, but I've had some great nights in bed.

Jimmy, 44, taxi driver

When I was young, struggling, and poor, no woman would have anything to do with me and I wanted sex all the time. Now I'm older and successful and I couldn't care less about sex. Women are attracted by my fame and they're always after my money and lifestyle. They want to be seen with me. I don't trust their motives or their intentions. Sex is useless to me. Power is much more attractive.

Clay, 30, investor/developer

How important is breathing, eating, or sleeping? Sex is just as important to me as any of the other necessities of life. I can't function without all of the above-mentioned items. So I guess sex is very, very important to me. Maybe I'm just vain.

Jessie, 21, clerk

4. Are you happy with your sex life?

Some days are happier than others.

Ben, 32, stock researcher

When my wife is happy, I'm happy. My wife is happy when our two-year-old is happy. So my sex life is basically controlled by a twenty-pound kid with soggy training pants. It is pretty sad.

Zack, 25, construction worker

I thought I was. I loved my girlfriend. We had sex weekly. We got along fine until I found some love notes she recently received from her girlfriend in college. I know the phrase "gay until graduation" sounds like a joke, but now I wonder. She says that she loves me, but I feel her passion is reserved for her former roommate. I'm confused, hurt, and still in love. I feel like I'm fighting an impossible foe. My sex life is great, but my love life is in the toilet.

Charles, 23, management trainee

What is a sex life? I presently don't have one, so, no, I'm not happy with my sex life. Where are all the girls when you need them? I'm away at school and all the girls I care about are back home. Somebody help me.

Michael, 19, student

5. What makes your sex life better than other people's?

My sex life is better because it's mine. I can only feel my own sensations, so my life is the only one I can know or experience. What I see as blue may not be what you see as blue. What I feel as pleasure, you may feel as pain. So I can only know what it feels like for me to climax and ejaculate. So in my frame of reference, which may in itself only be an illusion or a dream, my orgasm is the only one that matters.

Fred, 23, graduate student

My sex life is better 'cause, like Avis, I try harder. I work at it. I put effort in it. And I do my homework. I follow the Golden Rule, and I make others happy. I'm one of the good guys.

Robert, 29, telephone repairman

I work my ass off when I make love to my baby. There aren't a lot of things that I am great at, but doing the humpty is one thing I can do. I put in extra moves, I work and grind. I focus all my attention on the job at hand. And I deliver. I deliver long, hard, slow, and deep. I fill her up and over the top.

Terry, 22, unemployed

I am in between relationships right now. I have no sex life. A snail's sex life is probably better than mine.

Rodney, 48, electrician

6. If you could change anything about your sex life, what would it be?

If I had it to do all over again, I would have had more partners before I married my wife. I have loved my wife for fifty-five years, but it might have been nice to have had someone to compare her to sexually. In my day, you didn't have sex outside of marriage. I know guys have always bragged about their sexual conquests, but in my little circle of friends, most of us were virgins on our wedding night. Who were we going to have sex with? All the girls in town were friends and sisters and cousins of everyone else, so you couldn't find a "bad girl" who would let you do it with her. I couldn't have gotten laid in 1940 without a wedding ring on my finger if my life had depended on it.

Philip, 75, retired

I would focus more on the emotional than the physical. I think sex has become too much like exercise. I miss the emotional attachment, the hot, raging passion of my youth. I used to be really emotional and involved. I was consumed by love and romance and adventure. Now I feel like I'm in a rut. I do what is expected, but not much more. I miss the thrills of sex.

Barry, 43, personnel director

In theory I would have a sex life that is totally self-indulgent. If she couldn't keep up with me, I'd dump her and go on to the next notch on my bedpost. But in reality I'm a good guy and have only one love interest.

Boyd, 31, teacher

7. Who do you think has a better sex life than you, and why?

To hear my friends talk, all of them have a better sex life than me. But we all know talk is cheap, and as I can personally testify, so are their girlfriends.

Jed, 23, construction worker

I'm sure that rich people have a better sex life than me. They don't have to worry about bills, medical expenses, credit collectors. I have to work so hard just to keep food on the table and clothes on my kids. I don't have time to think about sex, much less do it. It is hard to plan sexy weekend getaways when you can't even keep the electricity on during the winter and your car is getting towed away.

Donnie, 26, laid-off factory worker

I've got to believe that movie stars, rock stars, and really rich people have a better sex life than me. When I hear some actor complain about what a rough time he has making it on five or six million dollars a year, I just want rip his throat out. Stop whining and enjoy the fantastic life you lucked into!

Paul, 36, construction worker

No one has a better sex life than me, because I work to make my own sex life. Hey, I'm not stupid, I let my wife think she's in charge, but no one makes my sex life but me.

Tony, 31, machinist

8. What is your special talent that makes you wonderful in bed?

My ability to wiggle my tongue with enthusiasm for hours makes me very popular with women. Long after my penis has given up and turned into a limping worm, my tongue is making women purr. I like the taste, the smells, the inner folds. I just love females.

Rick, 30, electrician

My dick is the best friend a woman can have. It is long, thick, dependable, and very low maintenance. All she has to do is suck on it a little bit and he will go for hours.

Reggie, 34, singer

My fingers make women melt. They go everywhere and release every tense muscle a lady has. Women quiver when I touch them with my special rubbing motion. I learned it in Boy Scouts.

Clarence, 29, energy consultant

My ability to really please a woman that is lucky enough to be in bed with me makes me wonderful. I aim to please and my stiff prick stays up for a very long time. I can go for hours until she is exhausted.

Tim, 34, editor

I am like the pink bunny, I keep going and going and going.

Troy, 36, saxophone player

9. What do you wish you were better at doing sexually?

I wish I could keep from climaxing so quickly. After wining, dining, dating, and seducing a woman, by the time I finally get into her panties, I'm overloaded and ready to come in a few minutes.

Jonathan, 22, machinist

I wish I could perform anal oral sex on my girlfriend without getting so squeamish. I have done it once before when I was really drunk, and she really, really loved it. But to tell you the truth, I was so drunk that if she hadn't made such a big deal out of it, I probably wouldn't even remember doing it. What seems like a bad dream for me has become her most favorite sexual moment. Tell me God doesn't have a sense of humor.

Keith, 30, lab technician

I wish I could go down on my girlfriend without gagging. I know I should love the smell and the taste of her cunt, but I simply don't. I've tried to learn to like it. I really have. I wish I could hold my nose sometimes and just dive in. I must be the one straight guy in the world who doesn't like to lick pussy.

Mel, 27, photographer

I wish I were better at reading a woman's thoughts and needs in bed. I mean, do we really know what they are thinking while we are pumping in and out of them? We know what they say, but is it the truth or just what they think we want to hear? We act like we know what they need but, do we?

Joe, 24, cabdriver

10. What's the first thing you notice when you meet a woman?

I'd like to say I notice her sparkling wit and abundant intelligence, but I really notice her tits and her mouth. Big tits and full lips can make up for a lack of clever conversation anytime.

Tyler, 42, research scientist

I notice her eyes and look to see if she is looking back at me. If she is interested in me, then my interest in her goes up a thousand percent. She becomes a goddess, simply the most beautiful woman on earth. If she ignores me, then she is an ugly, frigid bitch. Makes sense to me.

Jamie, 19, video store clerk

I notice her lips. Big, full, juicy, wet lips. Then I check to see if she has any teeth.

Barry, 24, cook

The first thing I notice about a woman is her face; it has to be nice to look at before I travel further down. If not, I look on. I guess I'm superficial in that respect. I mean, who wants to be seen with a dog?

Brian, 26, technician

11. Have you ever had any problems with sexual performance? If so, how did you handle them?

I became temporarily impotent after my girlfriend's six-year-old daughter accidentally kicked me in the testicles in a game of flag football. After ignoring the pain for two months, I finally went to the doctor for some antibiotics. By the time he finished squeezing my nuts and making me cough, I was almost ready to give up on the whole subject of sex. Fortunately, the swelling finally went down in my balls and went up in my penis.

Royce, 30, manufacturing inspector

I bent my penis once during sex when I was trying to get an extra fraction of an inch of friction. My penis bent, fell out, and hurt like hell. My girlfriend thought it was funny. I thought she was insensitive. That ended our love session that night. She wound up frustrated and in an ill mood. I told her that it served her right.

Sammy, 26, guitar instructor

Last week I fell asleep during sex with my longtime steady. We were both so tired, we didn't even say anything about it until the next night. I need a new life or something.

Tyler, 28, sports equipment retailer

No, I have never had a sexual performance issue. I would probably freak out if I were to have even a short-term problem.

Andrew, 33, lawyer

12. Are you sexually attracted to women much younger than yourself? If so, why.

What man doesn't like flat bellies, firm breasts, tight butts, and a total lack of excess emotional baggage? I don't care if she knows who the Beatles were. I can always let her listen to my CDs of golden oldies while we fuck.

Don, 35, pharmacist

There is a certain pleasure in being with women of your own age. Common experiences and shared backgrounds make conversation flow. Besides, it is too much work to train a young woman, when an older, more experienced woman has so much more to offer.

Anthony, 47, loan officer

The best situation would be to find the fountain of youth. I'd like to have the knowledge and experience of a fifty-year-old and the body of a teenager. Imagine the possibilities!

Kenneth, 55, historian

Physically it is exciting. Mentally it is depressing. More like a novelty than a serious relationship. The thrill is there, but the substance is lacking.

James, 43, college professor

I firmly believe that you should stay within your own age group. Too many problems arise when you date outside your age bracket.

Don, 23, construction laborer

13. How do you relate to much younger women?

With young women I concentrate on having fun and plain recreational sex. Girls want to have sex and a good time. It is very superficial, but that's fine with me. I impress them with money and good taste. I take them out on the town, buy them flowers, show them the finer things in life. I teach them about wine, fine dining, the theater. And I pay close attention to their needs when we make love. I work at making them climax in my mouth. I take my time. Since I can't compete with younger men's bodies, I don't even try. Single women my age are either angry, lonely, or just plain scary. Yes, we have much in common, but who cares? We might all have middle-age spread, but I don't want to compare notes. Give me a young, wet woman who doesn't want to blame me for everything that went wrong in her life.

Michael, 43, stockbroker

The relation with younger girls is simple. They want to have fun. So do I. It is that simple. I don't expect long-term commitments, and they certainly don't want them either. As long as we all understand the rules, everything is fine. The key is to have another one lined up when the current one starts wanting too much time, money, attention, commitment.

Raymond, 32, banker

Sex, period. That is about all we can relate to each other. If anyone says different, they are either lying or kidding themselves into being young again.

Randall, 58, retired

14. What do you think motivates men to date women twenty or so years younger than themselves? Is it mostly a sexual or physical attraction?

Older men date younger women because they can.

Mack, 49, store owner

An illusion of power. They see young women as trophies or rewards for hard work or a hard life. A young date brings back memories of good times, no hassles, lost youth. It makes for wonderful bragging rights on the golf course.

Jake, 50, golf trainer

Older men and younger women fill a fantasy need for both parties. Girls get money, security, knowledge, power, and long-lost daddies. Older men get to relive youth, feel the energy, touch the wet spots. The two go together. A young man with knowledge, money, and energy would be too much for any young girl to stand.

Bruce, 46, sales manager

I think older men date younger women because they want to return to their younger years, a second time around life, if you will. I think they are sick and should keep the sagging thing in their pants where it belongs.

Donald, 20, salesman

4 Methods

1. ***What is your favorite position?***
2. ***What is your partner's favorite position?***
3. ***What is your least favorite position?***
4. ***What is your partner's least favorite position?***
5. ***Which position do you use most?***
6. ***Who is in charge most of the time when it comes to having great sex—you or your partner?***
7. ***Can you climax in more than one position? Describe.***
8. ***What is the most unusual position you've ever tried?***

1. What is your favorite position?

I like my girlfriend's legs to be straight up in the air, wide-open, and receptive to my attention.

Gary, 20, cook

I like to take my wife in a standing position from behind. She bends over slightly against the canopy bed, and I enter her. I can make love without hurting my knees or straining my back. It makes me feel strong and virile.

Hank, 36, insurance adjuster

My favorite position has to be any one that has my girl ready, willing, and wet for me to stick my hard cock inside her . She could be standing on her head for all I care as long as she is wet for me.

Gus, 23, student

2. What is your partner's favorite position?

My wife likes to have a lot of variety in her life. Several years ago she literally made a list of different positions she wanted to try. She would check off each position on her master list and give it a rating. In spite of, or maybe because of, all our experimenting, she discovered that the basic missionary position was the most satisfying for her. She does like to rub her clitoris when I'm in her, so does that count as a variation on a classic?

Ivan, 35, sales representative

My girlfriend likes to be on the floor with her mouth open as I masturbate. The closer I get to climaxing, the closer she brings her lips to my penis. When I reach the point of explosion, she cups my testicles in her hands and clamps her lips around my penis. She swallows and gulps, and I twitch and spurt. It always makes me weak in the knees. She claims it helps keep her complexion clear and rosy. Whatever she thinks is fine by me.

Chris, 19, student

My lover's favorite position is from the rear. I get behind him and fill him to the brim. He loves it when I enter him hard and deep with my maleness. He screams for more. The harder I give it to him, the better he loves it.

Eddie, 24, fashion designer

3. What is your least favorite position?

My least favorite position is watching my bisexual girlfriend make love to one of her girlfriends. I feel left out, rejected, and alone. But after the other woman leaves, we always have intense sex, so in reality I guess it should be my favorite position.

Glen, 28, musician

Any position where I feel like I'm just a sex toy upsets me. I don't like doggy style because I can't see my lover's face. I could be a total stranger. She might like it, but it makes me feel cheap. Girls aren't the only ones who want to be loved for their minds as well as their bodies.

Reggie, 20, florist

I hate the straight missionary position. It's like not having any imagination to bring to the situation. I like variety.

Harley, 39, physician

4. What is your partner's least favorite position?

Any position that makes my girlfriend appear submissive to me makes her mad. Even if it feels good and makes her tingle, she won't let me do it more than once or twice. I believe her insecurity causes her to miss a lot of simple pleasure. If she wasn't so worried about perceived slights to her femininity, she might enjoy herself more.

Julian, 42, artist

My society girlfriend has become so refined, elevated, and image conscious that any position that involves passion, humanity, or natural body juices is taboo for her. She has become an ice princess, just like her girlfriends. I work. She spends. She has her social circle. I pay her bills. I'd like to take her to her tea party, throw her skirt up over her head, and bang the society right out of her in front of her snotty friends.

Dwight, 36, merchant banker

My partner is very open-minded. She will try anything that she thinks will feel good to her and me.

Ron, 32, salesman

5. Which position do you use most?

We use the missionary style the most because we like to kiss. We'd almost rather kiss than fuck. Maybe we are just traditionalists, but safe, old, reliable missionary-style sex works just fine with us.

Joe, 29, draftsman

I like the quickie approach. I like to hit and run and sweep her off her feet. My girlfriend likes lots of foreplay, tenderness, and attention to detail. Sometimes I like that approach. Sometimes I don't. Sometimes I just want to impale her on my prick and ram her. Maybe it is primal or genetic, or maybe I'm just a selfish dick. Yeah, that's probably it. Who am I kidding?

Edward, 28, photo technician

I don't use any position the most because I don't have sex. My girlfriend is going through a weird dry spell where all she wants to do is look at male porno on the Internet. I love her so I stay and put up with her, but I don't know how long we will continue to be together. She says she loves me, but I'm starting to wonder if it is true or not. She can masturbate anytime and thoroughly enjoy it, but she doesn't want me. Am I being a stupid fool or what?

Bobby, 37, data clerk

6. Who is in charge most of the time when it comes to having great sex—you or your partner?

My wife is certainly the key drive in our sex life. I could go weeks without having sex. She needs it several times a week. It just seems more important to her. She plans events. She comes up with new things to try in bed. I'm just a simple guy who likes straight in-and-out sex. She likes oils, feathers, gravity-defying positions. I think she watches too many talk shows on TV.

Gary, 46, deliveryman

I like to think that we're both in charge, but I probably am the one who makes the move most of the time. My wife is worried about the kids, the bills, dinner. I just want to goose her while she's cooking dinner. I spend all day thinking about being home with her, so by the time I get off from work, I'm ready to play. I hope we don't become boring old people and never do anything. I like the playfulness of our sex life.

Jack, 28, bricklayer

I am usually in charge. I have a very strong sex drive, she could care less about who the aggressive one is as long as I satisfy her.

Martin, 31, tool and die maker

7. Can you climax in more than one position? Describe.

I could climax in a straitjacket if I had to. Though friction does play a part most of the time, if I work on it, I can climax just by thinking real hard. I don't know if it is mind over matter, but it is certainly mind over sperm. I can recall a dozen childhood memories of wet spots on jeans in public places.

Larry, 19, student

I like to climax on my back, looking deep into the eyes of my girlfriend. I like to thrust up and hard into her body when I come. She holds my hands over my head and squeezes my legs with her thighs. I have the power, but she has the control. It is a nice balance of male and female.

Ned, 37, retailer

I can climax in any position. I can come inside or outside someone. I can come alone. I love to come. It is the greatest way of relaxing.

Dale, 26, unemployed

8. What is the most unusual position you've ever tried?

The most unusual position I've ever tried was the time my girlfriend sat on my lap at a college football game. We had our coats covering the juicy parts, but the combination of trying to make love and yet not draw attention to ourselves was exciting, but frustrating. I entered her easily enough. I just couldn't get much of a rhythm going without making her head bounce up and down and look silly. The fact that our team was completely outmatched and lost by forty-two points only added to the lack of enthusiasm from the crowd. Maybe they should have been trying their own positions out instead of watching the game. A good fuck should beat the wave as a crowd pleaser.

Harold, 38, auto parts sales manager

The most unusual position I've ever tried was in my girlfriend's swimming pool. We were at her parents' house for a cookout. While her dad grilled the hot dogs, and her mom fixed drinks for the friends, Julie and I just bobbed up and down on the side of the pool. We carried on a normal conversation with the rest of the family while my penis slid in and out of her slick vagina. I swear her little sister knew what we were doing, but she never said a word. The coolness of the water, combined with the fear of getting caught, made my orgasm that much more intense.

John, 20, student

The most unusual position I tried was when I let my girlfriend talk me into trying out some strange things sexually, which involved a peppermint stick, crackers, summer sausage, and banana peppers. I won't go into details, but it was one of the best nights of my sexual life.

Bradley, 34, contractor

5 Memorable Experiences

1. ***Describe the sexual experience that pushed all your buttons and threw you into a meltdown in record-breaking time.***
2. ***Describe the worst sex you've ever had.***
3. ***What was your strangest sexual experience?***
4. ***What was the messiest sex you've ever had?***
5. ***What was your most embarrassing sexual experience?***
6. ***Describe the longest sexual encounter you've ever had.***
7. ***Describe the shortest sexual encounter you've ever had.***
8. ***What was the biggest age difference between you and a lover?***
9. ***What was your funniest sexual experience?***
10. ***Describe the most sensual woman you have ever known.***
11. ***Was there ever the perfect woman for you who got away? If so, how?***
12. ***Has anything really bizarre ever happened to you in a relationship?***

1. Describe the sexual experience that pushed all your buttons and threw you into a meltdown in record-breaking time.

It may sound strange, but the best sex I ever had was the night I found out my wife was pregnant with our first child. We had been trying for over two years, and maybe I had put too much stress into the act of trying to conceive. I had just come home from work when she told me she had tested positive. We were so overjoyed, we embraced, slid to the living room floor, ripped each other's clothes off, and had strong, passionate sex. It was the personification of love and creation.

Jason, 35, electrical engineer

The hottest sex I've had happened when my girlfriend took all her clothes off in the living room while I was trying to watch a football game. She did a striptease. Got totally nude and proceeded to seduce me. I loved it. I'm not a jock, so she knew missing the game was no big deal. It was the fact that she just decided to take over the living room and make love to me that turned me on so much. It was wonderful. We tore the living room up. I dropped a full can of beer on the carpet and didn't even care. The next morning we found ranch dip under the coffee table, along with her panties. I think I like messy sex more than I realized.

Frank, 23, auto mechanic

The time I remember as being the outstanding sex of all time was when I went out with a girl I had met at work. She was drop-dead gorgeous and very smart, too. I asked her out and she hesitantly said to call her. I did and she agreed to go out with me. The first date was okay, but by the third week of dating she finally decided she would let me have my way with her. We had gone out to dinner and then to a club to dance. I guess we both had a little too much to drink. As we headed back to her apartment, she leaned over and whispered into my ear that if I wanted her, then I had to prove it. Now, that was a challenge I couldn't deny. I made it to her house in record time. We walked in and I grabbed her right at the front door and proceeded to rip her clothes off. My dick was so hard. I just had to have her. We fell to the floor and I devoured her as if there were no tomorrow. I drank of her as if I were a man dying of thirst. I rammed my dick into her hot vagina and we fucked until we were both exhausted. At this point we realized that the front door was still open and the sun was shining in. What a night that was. Oh, yeah, we are still together today.

Kenny, 36, teacher

2. Describe the worst sex you've ever had.

I was doing it doggy-style with my girlfriend. We had had too much to drink and eat, and I simply threw up all over her naked back. It went in her hair, all over the wall, and soaked the sheets. She was mad as hell, but at least I felt better.

Brad, 20, student

I can honestly say that the worst sex I ever had was with an ex-girlfriend who was exceptionally frigid. I could not get her to loosen up or relax for anything. She was unresponsive and cold. After many attempts to get her to relax and let go, we broke up over the horrible-sex issue. I hope she has learned to like sex, probably not though.

Jackie, 27, electrician

She was beautiful and erotic. Her hair smelled sweet, like honeysuckle, and I was completely attracted to her. Little did I know she was a he.

Nelson, 24, mortgage company manager

3. What was your strangest sexual experience?

The night my college roommate got drunk and gave me a blow job. We had been out clubbing, and we both struck out miserably. We couldn't get arrested, much less find dates. We drank tequila, whiskey, and beer all night. When we stumbled back to our dorm room, I vaguely remember screaming out how horny I was. My roommate made some wisecrack about how I should bend over and take it like a man. I told him to blow me. The next thing I knew, he had me pushed up against the wall, and my penis was in his mouth. It only took about five strokes before I exploded down his throat. He swallowed my juice, took another gulp of beer, and told me to shut the fuck up. The next day was just like all the others. I never said anything about what happened, and he didn't either. I never told him or anyone else to blow me again the rest of my college years.

Bert, 22, broadcast intern

My strangest sexual experience was when my girlfriend's mother tried to seduce me. She didn't succeed. Maybe she didn't really want to. I found the flirting highly erotic, even though she had never turned me on before. I think it was the idea of doing it with her that made me feel so horny. I left before anything went too far. But when I got home, she called me on the phone and started talking real suggestive to me. She told me to masturbate and tell her everything I was doing. I don't know why I did it, but I did. I worked myself to a climax and let her hear my groans. I know she was doing the same on her end of the line. I don't know why it made me so horny. It was just so weird.

Nate, 20, student

My strangest sexual experience was the first night with my new wife. I was so horny that by the time we were ready to screw, I started to enter her and came. Talk about exploding on impact. After a little while I was able to make love to her as a man should.

Johnny, 31, radio announcer

4. What was the messiest sex you've ever had?

It was on a Friday evening when I told my wife that I was hungry. She informed me that she would make me a dinner that I would not soon forget. I presumed, as I sat in the living room watching the tube, that she was fixing dinner. About thirty minutes later she called out to me from the bedroom to say dinner was served. I walked into the room and she had covered her body in all my favorite snack foods. I jumped right in and started eating her piece by tasty piece. We ended up with food all over the bed and the sex was the greatest, but messy.

Joey, 24, phone specialist

I was at college and terribly glad to be there. This would be my first experience at life away from home. I was now out in the big world by myself. The classes were hard, but I could handle it. I knew how to study and I knew how to get along with others. Girls were everywhere. Beautiful girls, sexy girls, willing girls. That's where I went wrong. I wasn't a virgin, but

I wasn't Don Juan. Tracey was perky and had a sharp wit and a great sense of self. She wasn't shy about anything, but I was. I was shy enough to make up for the both of us. She and I had decided to "do it" in my room, on a Saturday night. All the way. No turning back, no chickening out. The lights were down low, but there was enough light to see clearly. Man, I wish it had been pitch-black, but it wasn't. She didn't tell me she was on her period, and it scared the crap out of me. I knew girls had such things, but since I didn't have any sisters, I had never actually seen the results. I had been banging her hard, as requested, and blood was everywhere—I mean everywhere. I can't remember all that I said or did, but I know it came out all crazy and mixed up in my scared state of mind. She started laughing, and that really embarrassed me on top of everything else. *Messy* wasn't the word for it. It was horrible, like somebody got slaughtered or something, but I plan to try it again when I get up my nerve.

Don, 19, student

5. What was your most embarrassing sexual experience?

After three months of pursuing this hot little number from work, I couldn't get it up when the time came to score. Betty was a twenty-year-old coworker who had been friendly and flirty from her first week on the job. She was going through a messy divorce, needed a shoulder to cry on, and may have been looking for a father figure. I was over twice her age, but she said that after playing with boys, she was ready for a mature man. We schemed for weeks to actually get together. Our schedules kept conflicting, until we finally found a day when we both were in the same town, and on loose time charts. We decided to do an afternoon love session at the nearby business hotel where we normally put up our visiting clients. Since she handles the hotel reservations as a normal part of her job, it wasn't too difficult for her to book a room for a Mr. Peters from Miami, my hometown. I bought champagne, candy, and a silk nightgown. She looked so delicious when I opened the door to our love suite, I guess I just overloaded. We tried for an hour to get an erection. It seemed like a decade. I wanted her so bad, but I was limper than overcooked spaghetti. An older woman might have been understanding and sympathetic. Betty just gave up. She put her clothes on, took my presents, and laughed as she left the room.

Paul, 47, sales trainer

My most embarrassing sex experience was back when I was around twelve years old and had discovered my hand felt real good on my pecker. I was in the bathroom getting close to the edge, the door flew open, and my little sister along with a friend of hers came running in. I got so flabbergasted that I came out of sheer fright. They went running to Mom screaming that something was wrong with my pee pee cause yucky stuff was coming out on my hand. My parents realized what it was and started laughing hysterically while I almost died of embarrassment. They still tease me about it when I go to the bathroom at home.

Ross, 22, computer programmer

6. Describe the longest sexual encounter you've ever had.

The longest encounter I had was when I was too drunk to be screwing. I should have already passed out from the booze, but my girlfriend was wanting it, so I tried. The only problem was that once we got it up, it would not quit. We screwed for at least three hours and I could not come. I finally gave up and passed out, blue balls and all.

David, 26, store clerk

Longer than five minutes would be setting a record for me. My wife hates sex and I hate her.

Wayne, 58, retired machinist

7. Describe the shortest sexual encounter you've ever had.

When I was fifteen and on a trip to New York City with my parents, we stayed at a hotel on the edge of Central Park. Our second night there I sneaked out of the room and decided to do a little sight-seeing on my own. I walked over to Times Square. A tall, stunning black woman with incredibly long blond hair and a red push-up bullet bra came up to me and asked me if I wanted a date. I turned red, got an instant boner, and came in my pants. It was so awkward, yet emotional. I felt weak in my knees, embarrassed beyond belief, and happier than I could ever remember. It made life in our suburb of Louisville, Kentucky, seem tame by comparison. I can still recall every detail to this day, and it was over thirty years ago.

Jack, 48, psychiatrist

The shortest sexual experience I had was when I caught my manhood in my zipper. My girlfriend was in the backseat already out of her panties with her dress hiked up to her neck. I was in a hurry to join the action and pulled my zipper too quick, or something. The very tip of my uncircumcised penis got caught. It hurt like hell. I screamed. My girlfriend freaked out. The more I tried to get it out, the more it hurt. I finally jerked until my penis came out of the zipper. The tip was ripped and I was bleeding. My girlfriend was scared. I was the one bleeding, but she was the one who was scared.

Paul, 28, electrician

I've never had a short encounter, so I can't possibly answer this one.

Riley, 31, bartender

8. What was the biggest age difference between you and a lover?

If my memory is correct, she was eighteen and I was thirty-six. It was all strictly sex. We were coworkers and very lonely that night. She and I both knew what we were doing. It was a onetime thing and it never happened again, which is a shame. I have to say that the sex was out of this world.

Jason, 65, retired

I have never asked women how old they are. I've probably slept with women anywhere from the ages of twenty to sixty, and they were all wonderful. I love women and generally get along with them, sexually and otherwise. I couldn't care less how young or old they are provided they're adults.

John, 62, judge

A lady in her midsixties secured my services as an escort for one night. She was a society woman who actually needed an escort for a charity ball. Her husband was away, and she had to make an appearance. She was friends with my girlfriend's mother, and through the grapevine, the three of them decided that I would be an appropriate and safe escort for the event. She paid for my tux and the five-hundred-dollar benefit ticket. Though I make my living as a social worker, I can clean up into a fairly studly man. I had a great time putting on airs and cutting up on the dance floor. When the evening's event was over, she invited me in for a nightcap. We wound up having sex on her designer sofa. It wasn't the best or the worst I've had. I was more amazed at how she didn't feel that different from my twenty-three-year-old girlfriend when I closed my eyes. I just don't like knowing how much potential blackmail power she now has over me.

Brice, 26, social worker

9. What was your funniest sexual experience?

My girlfriend decided she was going to add some spice to our sex life by having me pour melting ice cream on her body. The idea was fine in theory, she just forgot that ice cream is cold, sticky, and messy. She was nude on our satin sheets, waiting for me to start the action. As soon as the ice cream touched her left breast, she jumped up and knocked the bowl out of my hand. The ice cream spilled all over the bed, and her two cats, Flo and Ernie, actually got in a fight, trying to see which one could lick up the most ice cream. The combination of cat fur, wet sheets, and goose bumps killed whatever romantic mood we might have had.

Jeff, 33, insurance salesperson

My girlfriend decided to play a tune on my skin flute. She made me hard, then she started humming on the end of my penis. She was singing a stupid nursery-school song about a big purple dinosaur. The whole moment seemed too weird for me to enjoy. I started laughing. She started laughing. I lost my erection. She got the giggles. After a few seconds of encouragement, I flipped her over and fucked the giggles right out of her.

Aaron, 25, housepainter

My funniest experience was when my hound dog became our birth-control device. It happened one night out in the cornfield with my girl. We were really having at it when my dog heard us moaning and decided to investigate the noise. He was a good hound dog, so he quickly found out what the noise was, but then he decided he wanted to join in. Here I was screwing this girl and the blame dog is trying to push me off so he could get involved. We started laughing so hard that we lost all sexual interest. What a showstopper. I'm just glad he didn't decide to take a bite out of my dick.

Brian, 24, rancher

10. Describe the most sensual woman you have ever known.

She is a woman I have never been sexual with, but would love to. I can't because she belongs to my best friend. This lady is so sensual that when she walks into the room, all eyes are automatically riveted on her. The way she walks, talks, and composes herself is so damn sensual it is unbearable at times. I know she doesn't do it on purpose, it just comes to her naturally. I would love to bury my face in her hair and her womanhood. I have dreamed of doing that very thing. I would never let her or my friend know how much I want her.

Gene, 34, tax collector

The one woman I remember the most was loving and patient but could not speak. She was mute. I loved her to death and would have married her, but she left me. I now have a wife who talks me to death. I wish sometimes I would slip on a banana peel and get some relief.

Harry, 77, retired banker

11. Was there ever the perfect woman for you who got away? If so, how?

I'm a hairstylist and I'm good at what I do. Women seem to like my cuts, and they like my looks. I've worn a wedding ring on my finger for years to keep women from coming on to me at the salon. I meet over a dozen assorted ladies each day, and if they all thought I was single, they'd just never leave me alone and let me get my work done. So I wear my mother's old wedding band and just do my job. One day I got a call to do hair and makeup on a music video being shot in town. The band was famous but not my cup of tea. I told the producer, whose wife is one of my regular clients, that I wasn't interested in trying to make middle-aged men look like teen idols. He told me the video was going to be filled with models and they were the ones who needed my help, not the band. The money was great, my expenses were paid, and I'd get to meet somebody besides pampered housewives. One of the models sincerely took my breath away. She was dressed to slink around on a custom hot rod, and they wanted me to make her up to look like your typical music-video slut. She had the most alluring lips, and a thin, world-class model's body that could sell ice to Eskimos. I fell head over heels for this divine creature. She loved the look I gave her. She laughed at my chitchat. She looked me straight in the eyes while I trimmed her bangs. She licked her lips while I teased her hair into the perfect fuck-me look. I kept her amused and touched up her stray locks between takes. At the end of the shoot I asked her if she would like to go to dinner and maybe hit a few clubs later. She told me that she would love nothing better and clasped my hands in a warm embrace. You know the rest. She saw my ring, had a fit, and cursed me out. She stormed off to her waiting limo and refused to take my calls at her hotel. I even had my producer friend try to call her up and tell her that I wasn't married, but she wouldn't take his message. She left town, I went back to my normal life, and I still see her photo in magazines every month or so.

Jere, 36, hairstylist

I was in love with my best friend's girl in college. He treated her like crap. She worshiped the ground he walked on. I loved her dearly. I believe now that if I had shown a little more interest in her, she would have been mine. I do know she wouldn't have married that jerk, had two kids, and then been left bitter and alone four years later. And I wouldn't be alone now thinking about her and what could have been.

Howie, 27, film producer

Since there is no perfect woman, I don't believe one ever got away. If you mean have I ever lost a woman, yes, who hasn't?

Phillip, 41, recording artist

12. Has anything really bizarre ever happened to you in a relationship?

Yes, I dated this lady for a while and we were remarkably in tune with each other. We knew what we each wanted or was going to say before a sentence was completed. At first I thought it was funny and interesting, in a weird sort of way, but it got to the point where we had nothing to say to each other. We eventually split up.

Todd, 40, graphic designer

Which moment? They're all bizarre. Women are bizarre. Life is bizarre. Hell, I'm bizarre.

Bobby, 46, codes inspector

I dated a woman who thought she was divorced. We had been living together for about two years when a police officer came to our door to serve divorce papers. She hadn't seen her husband in over eight years and didn't even really know what had happened to him. After she learned that she wasn't divorced from him, her attitude toward me changed almost overnight. She ended up leaving me two weeks later and moved back in with him. I hope they both rot in hell. They deserve each other.

Isaac, 37, taxi driver

6 Women

1. ***What type of woman turns you on?***
2. ***What type of woman turns you off?***
3. ***What do women need the most from a man?***
4. ***What do women want the most from a man?***
5. ***What do men need the most from a woman?***
6. ***What do men want the most from a woman?***
7. ***What do you envy most about a woman?***
8. ***What do you envy least about a woman?***
9. ***Can you communicate well with women?***
10. ***Can you be best friends with a woman without it involving sex?***
11. ***Women gold diggers. Do you know any, and if so, what do you think of them?***
12. ***How do you feel about women bosses? Do they challenge your ego or your manhood?***
13. ***Do you work well with women?***
14. ***Do you respect women?***
15. ***What do you think about women receiving less salary for the same positions men hold?***
16. ***Do you believe women mature earlier than men?***

17. Do you think women are unreasonable when they get distressed about how much time their husbands spend in front of the TV, at sporting events, or hanging out with the guys?

18. Have you ever defended a woman's honor?

19. Do you understand women?

20. Other than sexually or physically, are women very different from men?

21. Do you understand why they think the way they do?

1. What type of woman turns you on?

I like a woman with a sense of humor. Looks fade, so if a woman can't laugh at life, she will be unbearable. Besides, she would have to be able to laugh at things if she was remotely interested in me.

Sammy, 29, bartender

I like a true beauty queen. I like women who are stunning and so attractive that it hurts. I know a lot of guys say they want the girl next door. They settle for cute, pretty, nice. Not me. I want the girl who makes men stop in their tracks. I want the best, the fantasy girl. I find it as easy to love stunningly beautiful women as just everyday pretty girls.

Bobby, 34, photographer

It is hard to describe the type of woman that turns me on. There are several things about women that I consider a turn-on. Its not just her looks or how she comports herself—the lady could look like the girl next door and give me a slight wink and I'd melt before her eyes. Then there is the way she carries herself and takes care of herself that can be a real turn-on. I guess it all depends on the particular woman I meet.

Jed, 39, computer technician

2. *What type of woman turns you off?*

A very quick turnoff for me is the woman who thinks she is God's gift to man and we should bow down to her because she has graced us with her presence. What a bore!

Tony, 31, bouncer

Narcissistic. A mirror has its uses, but some women can't seem to live ten minutes without one.

Perry, 49, high school principal

I can't stand women who care more about their hair than their men. They should just shave their heads and get on with life.

Curtis, 20, pizza maker

3. *What do women need the most from a man?*

The women I've met need money, cash, stuff. They start out wanting love, affection, and attention. Then they need a little money for this or that. Soon I'm paying rent, buying groceries, arranging credit for installment loans. I'd rather get a whore and save myself the bother and expense of a so-called relationship.

Ricky, 40, taxi driver

Women need someone to tell them the truth. All of my problems with former girlfriends began with little lies. Once I lost their trust, the relationships were over. And what's worst, most of the lies were over stupid stuff that didn't really matter anyway.

Jeremy, 25, disc jockey

I think women need to be cherished and loved by the man that loves them. I am a true gentleman by nature.

Garth, 39, carpenter

4. What do women want the most from a man?

I believe women basically want the same things from men that men want from women—truth, honesty, friendship, a monogamous relationship, and lots of security.

Ben, 46, professor

Adoration, emotional support, and children. If I can just find my soul mate, I will give her these things and much, much more. Much more.

Mitch, 30, principal

Women want a hard dick and a wallet full of cash.

Joey, 19, bicycle mechanic

5. What do men need the most from a woman?

I want a woman to support me when I'm down and be there for me when things aren't so good. That is the true test. I'm purposely thinking of telling my girlfriend that I've lost my job and need to borrow some money from her, just to see her reaction. I need to know that she wants me for more than my ability to take her out to dinner four times a week. I need to see how she reacts to a few bumps in the road instead of our constant smooth sailing.

William, 25, songwriter

Faithfulness is extremely attractive to me. I'll put up with almost anything but sexual betrayal. With AIDS and everything, if my girlfriend strays, I could die.

Chuck, 20, student

Men need to be wanted and looked up to by a woman. They need to be shown that they are loved for themselves and not just for being the one that can support them. Men need to be shown that they are wanted, loved, and respected by their female counterparts.

Robert, 47, computer analyst

6. What do men want the most from a woman?

Sex and more sex. Hot sex, quick sex. Long slow sex. Just plain sex. Sometimes they want a friend or companion, but mostly sex.

Jordan, 32, clerk

Pussy.

Lionel, 32, roofer

I want a lover, companion, friend, and a cunt so tight it brings tears to my eyes when I fuck her.

Vito, 27, chef

7. What do you envy most about a woman?

I envy and resent that a woman can blame bad behavior on PMS and her upcoming periods. She could wipe out an entire nation and get away with it by blaming it on her special friend.

Donnie, 24, waiter

I love pussy. I can never get enough, so I guess I envy a woman because she always has her own, just down there wet and waiting. It must be great.

Trevor, 18, student

I am in awe of the ability to give birth. I know this isn't a big sexy answer or probably smart-ass enough for a typical guy's response, but I really envy a woman's ability to bring new life to the planet. And I do like large breasts very much.

Jack, 24, graphic artist

I envy a woman's ability to whine or be real sexy and get just about anything she wants from a man. We men are weak and cannot say no to the women we love. Besides, the woman can cut us off from our sexual needs.

Frank, 39, gardener

8. What do you envy least about a woman?

Having to wear dresses and high heels in the wintertime. How do they stay warm? I also don't envy all the facial and hair things they put themselves through to look good.

Chris, 25, graduate student

Women carry the hearts of children and men deep within them. They nurture and teach generation after generation.

They are underpaid and go through life getting little thanks. Men get away with all they can and women suffer.

Warren, 50, photographer

I never have to worry about my tits sagging when I get old. For that I am truly thankful.

Vincent, 42, butcher

9. Can you communicate well with women?

I have mastered the art of fake sincerity. I can overwhelm women with my subtlety. I can overpower them with my sensitivity. I can bullshit my way through conversations, relationships, and life. Women love me, until they get to know me. And vice versa, I might add.

Richard, 40, office manager

I look straight into a woman's eyes and tell her what she wants to hear. It never fails. I'm such a prick most of the time.

Sal, 37, lawyer

If a woman really wants to listen to me, then, yes, I can communicate with her. I find most women just want to play mind games and screw you over.

Barry, 30, bartender

I can communicate well with women and men. Being a motivational speaker makes it is easy to overlay this into everyday conversations. I took a course in college to overcome my inability to talk one to one with people.

Lee, 45, motivational speaker

10. Can you be best friends with a woman without it involving sex?

Absolutely. In my field of work, I meet more women than men, so naturally most of my friends are women. Females are easier to talk with.

Cody, 21, hairdresser

It's hard, but then so am I, most of the time.

Seth, 37, check-cashing business

What's the point? It's a waste of good pussy.

Joe, 19, student

11. Women gold diggers. Do you know any, and if so, what do you think of them?

Gold-digging women come and go in my life. Maybe I just ask for it somehow, but it seems that most women will not only allow but actively encourage a man to spend all of his money on making their lives better. They want better cars, more clothes, newer gadgets, finer things. And that is all well and good, but they seem to expect me to pay for it all. I'm sick of it. I'm gonna get me a dog.

Bob, 43, plumber

I figure women have such a tough time in life that any gold they can manage to hold onto is fine with me. I know the women in my life earned every dime they ever squeezed out of me.

Fred, 38, electrician

As long as I know going in that money is the real goal, I'm okay with it. The thing that gets me is when a woman talks about love, emotions, romance, and commitment, and I find out she is only interested in getting my gold card.

Dan, 46, architect

I married the one gold digger that ever came on to me. She thought I had a lot more money than I really did. Her girlfriend told her I was rich. We had been dating for a few months before she realized I was broke. By then it was too late. My overpowering wonderfulness had conquered her. We've been happily married ten years, and she actually makes more money at her job than I do.

Gil, 30, technical writer

Unfortunately, men have turned a lot of women into gold diggers. They will not tell a woman no. Since the beginning of time men have treated women with less respect and equality than other men. I do not appreciate gold diggers but they do seem to get the nicer things in life.

Danny, 37, insurance sales

12. How do you feel about women bosses? Do they challenge your ego or your manhood?

Personally they don't bother either my ego or my manhood as long as they know what they're doing. If they got the position fair and square and did not sleep their way up the so-called ladder, then great.

Raymond, 29, service technician

Women never challenge my manhood. Not in the workplace, anyway. I find women bosses, and I've had some, more fair than men bosses. Women are generally more creative and innovative, they are calmer and definitely not as arrogant. I really enjoyed the women bosses I had, and I never slept, or tried to sleep, with any of them.

H.B., 49, architect

As long as they treat me fairly, I don't care. I can get along with any reasonable person.

Alan, 34, traffic cop

13. Do you work well with women?

I love working with women. They are nice to look at. They smell good. Their voices sound pleasant. And I can always imagine that I'm going to get lucky with them in bed someday. You never know, it could happen!

Gene, 28, short order cook

I work in broadcasting, and all the women here are so busy trying to become the next network superstars, they don't even know I exist. I'm not even a rung in their ladder to the top. I'm more like the lint in their navels.

Barry, 23, tape operator

Most of the women I work with are true friends, and I would work anywhere with them. I am very easygoing and get along well with the opposite sex.

Keith, 21, salesclerk

14. Do you respect women?

My mother taught me to respect her, as well as other women. I always listen to my mother. I'm not a mama's boy in any way, but I firmly believe in respecting others.

Doug, 34, air-conditioning repairman

Good grief, yes, I respect women. How would any man ever get any if he didn't? Do I respect my sexual needs? Yep. I'm not stupid. I know not to bite the hand that fucks me.

Xavier, 50, home builder

If she wants my respect, she has to earn it. I don't make any special allowances just because she squats to pee.

Leo, 45, government clerk

15. What do you think about women receiving less salary for the same positions men hold?

I think it sucks, especially since I spend most of my wife's money as it is. If she could make more for doing the same job, that would put more money in my pocket. That I would like.

Pete, 27, unemployed

My wife makes more money than I do because we both are in sales and work on commission. She is able to flirt and play with customers, and it shows in her paycheck. I put in the same hours and earn about half what she makes. I don't think it's particularly fair, but what can I do about it?

Ralph, 32, real estate sales

I know you're going to call me a male chauvinist pig, but I think there are some jobs that women are not qualified to do. If they have those jobs, then, yes, they should receive less pay.

Mathew, 56, mechanic

16. Do you believe women mature earlier than men?

Hell, yes, it's been proven time and time again. They seem to know what to do and how to do it earlier than men. I take my hat off to women.

Louis, 29, nurse

It's all a charade. We're all crazy, we're all messed up, and we're all immature little people running around in grown-up bodies. The whole fucking world should be locked up, to tell you the truth. That's all I can say.

Tony, 31, dance instructor

I believe a one-hour-old newborn female is more mature than her identical male twin, and she stays ahead for the rest of her entire life.

Jack, 28, desktop publisher

17. Do you think women are unreasonable when they get distressed about how much time their husbands spend in front of the TV, at sporting events, or hanging out with the guys?

If my wife would just try to like football, we would have a better life together. She knew I was a fan when we dated. Why should she think that just because we got married, I'm going to stop watching sports on TV? I wish she'd join me on the sofa sometime instead of having a fit in the kitchen.

Ralph, 27, driver

My girlfriend is a basketball freak. She knows the stats, the teams, the rankings, everything. I thought she was just playing along when we first started dating, but now she is the one glued to the tube with a bottle of wine and some chips. She knows lots more about the game than I do.

Ernie, 22, deliveryman

My wife is just as big a sports fan as I am. We love to go to the games, and we use the hours in front of the TV to have our quality time together. I don't hang out with the guys unless she is right beside me. I know of a lot of other guys that have problems with their wives. If they would spend a little bit of time with them, they would be happier, too.

Alex, 34, collection recovery

18. Have you ever defended a woman's honor?

Yes, but only a couple of times in a bar. I guess I'm one of those guys who believes a girl should be able to go into a bar without being thought of as an instant pick-up by the first jerk who can get to her table. If guys can stop for a drink to unwind, why can't a girl?

Derek, 32, clinician

The night I lost my two front teeth I thought I was defending a woman's honor. The big fucker was slobbering all over her dainty red dress while she was unsuccessfully trying to fight him off. The pop band playing in the corner just kept on playing through all the screaming. People in the room were ignoring her plight, and slobber-puss just kept on pawing at her. I couldn't stand it, so I went over to do something. Twenty minutes later and two teeth less than I used to own, I'm sitting in jail with this son of a bitch and he's looking at me like I'm his midnight snack. Turns out little red-dress riding hood wouldn't press charges against him. How was I supposed to know this asshole was her husband?

Keith, 37, property manager

When I was seven years old, my next door neighbor called my sister a "stinking thief." I hit him in the face and he busted my lip. I bled all over him and myself. It turned out that my sister had put on makeup and perfume and stolen a kiss from him in our backyard. She thought he was cute. I haven't come to her rescue since.

Calvin, 28, tree surgeon

19. Do you understand women?

I don't understand how I turn on my TV and there are pictures and sound coming out of a black box. So why in the hell do you think I have a clue when it comes to women? I understand that I can never understand them, and I don't even want to anymore.

Frank, 39, pilot

I don't know of any man that honestly understands a woman. I think that is one of the reasons they are so appealing.

Bart, 26, animal trainer

20. Other than sexually or physically, are women very different from men?

They are definitely different. They are more emotional, rational, and forgiving and just quicker at a lot of things than men. They are sensible, nurturing, lovable; besides, they are easier to look at than men. I believe a woman would make a great president.

Allen, 22, salesclerk

You better believe it, and if you don't, you're in for a hell of a ride! Women are emotionally stronger, more flexible to change, have stronger stomachs (they don't start hurling when trying to change Junior's diaper), and they definitely possess greater ability to love unconditionally. For us men, that's a gift from heaven. Think what god-awful trouble we men would be in if women were just like men.

Todd, 42, radio programmer

Women "forget" when it's convenient, "hear" when they're sleeping, and "cry" whenever it suits their needs. No guy I know could get away with a tenth of the games women play.

Barry, 24, draftsman

21. Do you understand why they think the way they do?

I don't. Just when I think I have a clue, something happens that blows my entire theory out of the water. It is hard to be optimistic in dealing with the female mind. Even when I start trying to second-guess my original beliefs, it backfires in my face. So basically, why bother? I just accept the futility of the task.

Randy, 20, philosophy major

I don't buy into this pop psychology about men are from one planet and women are from another. That might sell books, but my basic approach to understanding women, and in fact, people in general, is to follow the lessons of another book, the Bible. I've found the Golden Rule is just about the best guide to everything I attempt in life.

George, 26, bookseller

I gave up trying to figure women out when I was ten years old. I have six sisters.

Anthony, 28, drummer

7 Body Parts

1. *What do you love about a vagina?*
2. *What do you not like about a vagina?*
3. *What do you love about a penis?*
4. *What do you not like about a penis?*
5. *Do you think a man's chest plays an important role in great sex?*
6. *What do you consider the most attractive part of the female anatomy?*
7. *What do you consider the least attractive part of the female anatomy?*
8. *What do you consider the most attractive part of the male anatomy?*
9. *What do you consider the least attractive part of the male anatomy?*
10. *Does a small vagina feel much more pleasurable?*
11. *Where is your sexual hot spot?*
12. *How does it affect you to see your partner developing wrinkles and other normal signs of aging?*
13. *Do you think women show these signs of aging at a faster pace than men?*
14. *What do men call their penis?*

15. What do men call a vagina? How do you refer to women's breasts?

1. What do you love about a vagina?

I love everything about a vagina. I've spent my entire life trying to get back into one ever since I popped out of my mother's.

Spencer, 34, recording engineer

The eternal wetness of it.

Larry, 20, student

I love the way a vagina wants to hold on to my penis and milk it dry.

Jim, 25, industrial designer

I like the fact that it is totally hidden, and you can only experience its pleasure by trusting your penis to it's secrets.

Gerald, 45, pharmacist

I love the way it makes my dick all stiff and hot. I like the friction and firm walls around me. What can I say? I simply love being inside my girl's vagina.

Keith, 24, truck service

2. What do you not like about a vagina?

I don't really like the way they bleed every month. I don't like the emotional roller coaster they call PMS—I call it being a bitch. And sometimes it smells rather pungent. Other than that, I pretty much like it.

Samuel, 18, fast-food cook

Yeast infections, that cottage cheese stuff. I haven't been able to eat cottage cheese since I was twenty-three. How gross. I still don't understand why women get those infections. I just try to be loving and steer clear when she has one. I've never told her I thought it was disgusting, but she's probably figured it out on her own.

Brian, 29, roofing contractor

I don't like the fact that a sharp piece of glass or a razor blade could be hiding up inside one, just waiting to get revenge.

Grant, 32, bookseller

3. What do you love about a penis?

I love the way it makes me happy. I like the excitement it brings to women. I like the intense pleasure it gives me when I ejaculate. I like the fact that I can hold it, shake it, play with it, even bend it sometimes. It is probably my best body part, and maybe my one true friend.

Roger, 26, customer service representative

I like how a hard dick can get the attention of women. An erection cuts right through the bullshit and goes right to the thing that matters: sex.

Bill, 19, student

I like how powerful it feels when it is hard and ready. I feel strong, alive, and vital. The blood captured in my penis makes me dizzy, and my heart races. I feel like I am capable of amazing feats. I'm just amazed how quick the feeling disappears once I climax. Then all I want to do is take a nap.

Carter, 34, salesman

I like the idea that I don't have to pull my pants down to take a leak. Mainly I like the fact that it can give two people so much pleasure—me and the one I'm with.

Mel, 38, machinist

4. What do you not like about a penis?

I don't like the fact that I can't hide an erection and they come at the most inconvenient times. Such a curse. Women are lucky they can disguise their excitement.

Dewayne, 24, waiter

I don't like it when the wind blows across my dick, makes me hard, and people look at me funny. There's usually not a good-looking chick within a mile, so I look like a pervert.

Sean, 25, restaurant manager

When my penis refuses to get an erection, despite lubrication, attention, and encouraging words, I'd just as soon cut it off and flush the thing down the crapper.

Reuben, 45, corporate tax specialist

5. Do you think a man's chest plays an important role in great sex?

My girlfriend loves to grab the hair on my chest and bite my nipples when we have energetic sex. She seems to forget that they're attached to my body. I don't have too many spare nipples put back for a rainy day.

Carl, 25, house inspector

I'm a gay man and I know how important a smooth, hairless chest is to me. I love a strong, toned male chest heaving over my face as I take my lover deep down my throat. I put my hands straight up into the air and pinch his nipples until he explodes.

Richie, 30, insurance adjuster

I don't really think about my chest during sex. My girl loves to rub my chest while we are doing the hokey-pokey. She says a strong chest is a turn-on for her, so I don't complain.

Joseph, 34, weight lifter

6. What do you consider the most attractive part of the female anatomy?

I am a breast man. A woman's breast is the most beautiful part of her body. Give me a girl with firm, perky boobs and I'm in seventh heaven.

Glen, 26, photo processor

My dick, when it's hooked deep into my wife.

Jeff, 35, auto industry representative

A full mouth with dark red lipstick is my image of heaven. Throw in a hot, darting tongue, and I soon need a clean pair of boxers.

Reginald, 40, tailor

I know I sound like a bumper sticker, but the most attractive part of any woman really is her brain. With smarts, she can make anything look good. Without brains, great looks just fade into stupidity. Who really wants to spend a lot of time with a bimbo once the sex is over?

Joel, 36, investor

7. What do you consider the least attractive part of the female anatomy?

I think a woman's vagina is the least attractive part. It looks like something dead you'd find washed up on the beach. Why do you think they wait until a boy turns at least twelve years old before they tell him about sex? If they showed six-year-old boys where babies come from, elementary schools across the nation would explode from the bloodcurdling screams of terror. It takes years of brainwashing to convince males that vaginas are good things.

Hank, 35, custodian

A big mouth and an empty brain are two of the least attractive parts of a woman.

Freddie, 32, auto detailer

A saggy stomach really turns me off. I think a woman should work a little and keep her gut flat and toned. If I can do a few sit-ups, anybody can.

Ronnie, 24, salesman

Feet, definitely the feet. Some women have ugly feet. They wear sandals and sexy heels. Yuck.

Donald, 19, lab technician

8. What do you consider the most attractive part of the male anatomy?

A flat stomach with rippling muscles. A man can have skinny legs, no arm muscles, but if he has a flat, strong stomach he can still get plenty of girls. Go figure.

Jody, 23, bartender

A guy's manhood in full erection is a sight to behold. The reason some societies worship the penis and have huge marble statues erected in the shape of dicks is because it makes perfect sense. Who wouldn't worship a big, permanent hard-on?

Brett, 20, tour guide

My best part is my winning smile and my goofy face. I have smiled my way into more ladies' panties than you would probably believe.

Zane, 32, barber

9. What do you consider the least attractive part of the male anatomy?

I think an unaroused penis is pretty pathetic looking. It just hangs and leaks and smells. So, I try to keep mine in a full state of erection at all times. I consider it my aesthetic duty. Am I a great guy, or what?

Terry, 25, graphic artist

Most of my friends' attitudes are pretty unattractive when it comes to treating women right. They lie, they cheat, they use women up. I don't like it, but I don't do anything to stop them, so I guess I'm as bad as they are.

Al, 21, automobile stereo installer

I think my butt hole is pretty damn ugly. And my girlfriend agrees with me. She will not let me walk around naked, even in our bedroom with the door closed.

James, 27, baker

A man's face with an eight-o'clock shadow on it. How can you get close to your girl if she flinches every time you touch her with your face?

Jordan, 36, telemarketer

10. Does a small vagina feel much more pleasurable?

I guess if you have a small dick, it is more pleasurable. If you have a normal-size dick, then it doesn't matter, unless she is stretched from having several kids. If so, then hopefully she is with the father of the kids.

Reginald, 30, lawn gardener

I have yet to find a small vagina. The ones I've been in start out okay, and then just seem to fall apart. After about five minutes I feel like I'm waving my penis in a big, dark pit. Give me a tight butt hole and let me do my thing.

Chad, 26, dance instructor

In my case, my well-endowed penis was too big for my former petite girlfriend. I caused her so much pain just trying to enter her, we always got into horrible fights. She loved foreplay with my tongue and my finger, but when it came time to put the beast in, she'd lose all interest. We just weren't physically compatible.

Ethan, 39, boxer

11. Where is your sexual hot spot?

My sexual hot spot is in the rim of my uncircumcised penis. When I am erect, the bulging purple head of my dick is master control center. If I am having intercourse, it is the friction on the rim that keeps me going. If I am receiving oral sex, it is the attention my girlfriend directs toward my rim that makes me want to love her the rest of my life. That such a small area should have such importance is probably just another case of ironic justice.

Ernie, 38, diamond broker

My favorite hot spot is my tongue. When my girlfriend grabs my tongue in her mouth and sucks it hard and deep into her mouth, I go nuts. She holds on tight and won't let me have my tongue back. It hurts a little, but I love it.

Andrew, 31, computer programmer

I have several hot spots, but my most sensitive area is my ear. When a girl sticks her tongue inside my ear, I melt. I want to eat her alive.

Ernie, 29, interior decorator

12. How does it affect you to see your partner developing wrinkles and other normal signs of aging?

As long as she can accept my aging process, I am okay with hers. I love my wife for who she is, not what she looks like.

Kevin, 49, store owner

I don't like it when women show heavy signs of aging. See a plastic surgeon. If it's my wife, then I'll even pay for it. I want a sexy woman, not a hag.

Joe, 48, paramedic

I don't mind the wrinkles as much as I object to her efforts to hide them. There is nothing as silly as a fifty-year-old woman pretending she is still twenty-five. Attitude is one thing, but reality is so much more convincing.

Perry, 56, supervisor

13. Do you think women show these signs of aging at a faster pace than men?

Yes. But women seem to accept the fact and are willing to spend billions of dollars for cosmetics, plastic surgery, and diet books to keep up the illusion. If women accepted their appearances and the inevitability of aging, the entire economy would probably go into the Dumpster.

Arnie, 45, corporate lawyer

African-American women and Asian women retain their youthful looks longer than Caucasian women. I once dated a black lady who told me she was twenty-five, and I later discovered she was forty-eight. And you know, it didn't matter to me one bit. On the other hand, I've seen white women in their thirties with leathery skin from years of sun poisoning who looked twenty years older than they were.

Doug, 30, reporter

Not all women show signs of aging that fast. Women who take care of themselves look years younger than they are. I admire that in a woman.

Gary, 37, land surveyor

14. What do men call their penis?

I don't know what other men call theirs, but I've called mine anything from my rod, my shaft, dick, pecker, pole, kitty detector, to just what it is, a penis.

Daniel, 32, bricklayer

Dick. What else is it?

Billy, 25, physician assistant

I call my penis "Bubba, the legendary Squirt Monkey."

Troy, 20, student

I call my pecker My Best Friend, because he is.

Arlo, 37, shoe repairman

I used to call him Old Faithful, now I just call him Old.

Dexter, 47, video technician

15. What do men call a vagina? How do you refer to women's breasts?

I call my girlfriend's vagina the bottomless pit and her breasts ihops, short for our favorite restaurant, the International House of Pancakes.

Buddy, 29, deliveryman

My baby's private part is known as the honey pot. Winnie the Pooh would kill for a taste of this stuff. I call her breasts my ear muffs. They keep me warm on winter nights.

Jamie, 20, data clerk

I call every woman's female part her cunt. I like the sound of the word and the way it gets such a strong reaction out of people. I can be all sweet, cuddly, and romantic, and I say the C-word, and the whole mood changes. Words are powerful, and I like to play with people's reactions.

Josh, 23, projectionist

I call my wife's vagina her love muffin or hot box, sometimes even the sugar shack. I call her breasts either boobs, honkers, or tits.

Darien, 24, singer

I used to call my latest girlfriend's private part the name of whoever I was dating just before I started dating her. It was my little private joke. Then it backfired on me. My current girlfriend, Susie, with her pussy, "Mary," heard a message on my answering machine from Mary, saying her wet, dripping "Susie" really missed me. I was fucked and left nameless.

Floyd, 30, athletic instructor

8 Masturbation

1. ***Do you masturbate?***
2. ***How do you masturbate?***
3. ***Where do you masturbate?***
4. ***How often do you masturbate?***
5. ***What do you think about when you masturbate?***
6. ***Do you feel comfortable when you masturbate, or do you feel as if you are doing something naughty?***
7. ***Do you consider masturbation an important part of your sex life?***
8. ***Have you ever masturbated in front of your partner? Did it have an effect? Describe.***

1. Do you masturbate?

I have been choking my chicken for ten years, and I don't plan to stop until they put me in the grave.

Cecil, 23, automotive stereo installer

I masturbate to remain faithful to my girlfriend. By keeping my testicles drained, I don't get the urge to cheat on my steady. I spill my seed about four times a week and have intense sex with her the other three days. It helps keep me sane and less horny.

Bernard, 19, student

The only time I masturbate is when my girl is on the rag, or if she wants to see me masturbate. It seems to turn her on to watch me.

Ben, 27, graphic artist

2. How do you masturbate?

I start out imagining my girl performing oral sex on me, then I let my hand do the rest. It is a great stress reliever.

Peter, 21, comedy writer

I use my hand, of course.

John, 36, fireman

A washable, fur-lined winter glove can be a man's best friend, if you know what I mean.

Mel, 45, concrete specialist

I like to lean against the wall of the shower and stroke myself while the hot water washes away all my sweat. I use a soapy washrag and scrub away my tension.

Walt, 26, deliveryman

3. Where do you masturbate?

I jerk off in my car on the way to and from work. I keep a pair of my girlfriend's panties in my seat and use it to catch my spunk. I haven't washed them in about six months.

Randy, 27, cellular phone salesperson

Like most red-blooded men, I jerk off in the shower every night.

Stephen, 20, custodian

I usually masturbate when I'm horny and not with a girl. It doesn't matter if I'm in the bathroom, kitchen, or wherever. I can jerk off anywhere.

Everett, 34, investigator

4. How often do you masturbate?

Only when necessary to relieve myself in a dry spell.

Larry, 27, shoe sales

I masturbate at least every other day. It makes me easier to get along with. It's my de-stressor.

Roy, 29, horse jockey

It has been five years since I had sex or ejaculated. It just isn't that important to me. I would have thought that I would have exploded by now or died from the pain, but my sperm seemed to disappear along with my sex drive after my divorce.

Oscar, 39, lab technician

5. What do you think about when you masturbate?

I think about the most incredible pair of lips wrapping around my penis. I imagine a beautiful pair of intense sky-blue eyes staring up at me, through a silky, golden mass of bangs. She has a cute little turned-up nose and a mouth that could suck the chrome off a bumper.

Greg, 28, radio announcer

When I jerk off, I dream about the waitresses I work with. All day long they flirt and tease me, yet I know none of them would ever go out on a date with me. They all see me as their "favorite little brother." I wish they could see me for the man I am. Until then, I'll fall asleep at night dreaming about the things I want to do to them.

Dudley, 19, busboy

I dream about movie stars, singers, and supermodels when I pound my pud. I dream that I am in the middle of a pussy mountain of wet, willing bodies, each woman trying to make me happier than the next.

Aaron, 21, pre-med student

I'm lucky, I don't have to masturbate. But if I did, I would imagine this drop-dead gorgeous chick sucking me off wearing red lipstick on her full pouty lips.

Rufus, 21, men's specialty sales

6. Do you feel comfortable when you masturbate, or do you feel as if you are doing something naughty?

If you are truly comfortable with your sexuality, then it can't be naughty. If it feels good, do it. If you are uncomfortable with masturbating, then you can't be open with your lover.

Harry, 32, auto sales

I always fear getting caught by the women in my life. It used to be my mom, then my girlfriends, now my wife. It doesn't stop me from beating my meat, but the fear of getting caught is always on my mind.

Jasper, 40, tax adviser

I feel like I'm getting away with something, and that is part of what makes me horny.

Todd, 18, student

7. Do you consider masturbation an important part of your sex life?

Masturbation gives me the power to control my sex life. I don't have to put up with grief, aggravation, or nonsense just because I'm horny. Knowing this, I find I can concentrate more on the actual relationship than just being driven by the sex. When you take lust and the need to ejaculate out of a relationship, things become much clearer.

Mel, 30, computer technician

If I didn't jack off regularly, I'd probably go nuts. I get so worked up and horny sometimes, I just have to get off by myself and get some relief. I like sex with women better, but you can't always find a girl to go to bed with when you need one.

Terry, 23, mechanic

Not so important that I forget to give pleasure to my girlfriend. But, if she's not in the mood, then I have no qualms about relieving myself of a massive hard-on.

Ross, 38, massage therapist

8. Have you ever masturbated in front of your partner? Did it have an effect? Describe.

Yes, I am not ashamed to admit it. At first she didn't like it, but as I urged her on, she definitely got into it. I got even more turned on watching her as she watched me jerk off. She kept licking her lips as if she wanted some of it, yet she didn't want me to stop what I was doing. We were both very hot. We ended up having one of the best sexual experiences of our lives together. It was great.

Tommy, 25, machinist

My girlfriend caught me when she walked in the bathroom last week without knocking. She didn't say anything, but she did look pretty disgusted. I felt like I was thirteen years old again.

Kevin, 30, software designer

9 Oral Sex

1. ***Do you like giving oral sex? Under what circumstances?***
2. ***Do you like receiving oral sex? Under what circumstances?***
3. ***Do you like to give and get at the same time (69)?***
4. ***What is your favorite part of giving oral sex?***
5. ***What is your favorite part of getting oral sex?***
6. ***Do you like to have your mouth on your partner's vagina when she is climaxing?***
7. ***Is it important to you that your mate swallow?***
8. ***Do you swallow?***

1. Do you like giving oral sex? Under what circumstances?

I love to give head. I like the power I get from thrusting my tongue into a warm, wet woman. I like the naughty nature of it. I love the smell, the heat, and the taste. I like it when a woman has thick juice and overwhelms me with her musk. I will perform oral on the woman I love anytime, anywhere. All she has to do is ask.

Travis, 32, medical technician

I love to suck a hard penis until it chokes me with sperm. My hetero friends can't understand why I like it so much, but I tell them to turn off the lights and I'll explain everything. They act all scared and grossed out, but I know that all of them would love my mouth, and half of them might even ask for seconds.

James, 27, stained-glass craftsman

I started giving women head to show them that I cared about their pleasure. Then I discovered that I really liked the taste of their juices. So now I suck them for my own pleasure.

Edward, 20, fast-food server

I will only perform oral when I know the woman is freshly showered. I'm sorry, but I have a very weak stomach. If her natural odor is a bit overwhelming, how can I give her the pleasure she so richly deserves? If she is clean, I can perform oral for hours and not get enough.

Randy, 24, student

2. Do you like receiving oral sex? Under what circumstances?

I can have oral performed on me anytime, anywhere. I simply love the way my wife sucks and licks my manhood. She seems to enjoy it just as much as I do.

Tim, 31, equipment sales

I would let a vacuum cleaner suck me dry if I wasn't afraid of hurting my male member. I love a good suck.

Stuart, 40, bus driver

When my lovers takes the time to bring me to arousal, licks my shaft, and plunges my erection down her throat without choking, I always climax in great gushes of appreciation.

Barney, 27, dance instructor

I'm the only guy I know who doesn't like oral sex. Maybe I just have a real fear of urine. I don't like to give or get oral sex. The thought of letting my girlfriend kiss me after she has had my penis in her mouth makes me ill. I don't care what people think. It just seems like something a whore would do.

Paul, 30, printer

3. Do you like to give and get at the same time (69)?

I hate it when my girlfriend wants to do 69. The closer she gets to climax, the less attention she pays me. She gets to climax, while I get to ache in my nuts. She usually has to completely finish her orgasms and rest awhile before she gets the energy to come back and satisfy me.

Jeremy, 27, physical trainer

I like the frenzy of a good, energetic session of 69. My girl follows my rhythm and matches me lick for lick. It is the best ride I've ever been on. We usually explode at the same time and swallow as much as possible.

Barry, 40, insurance executive

Yes, yes, and definitely yes. We can 69 every night. We both really enjoy giving each other pleasure in this way. Sometimes we compete to see who will last the longest. She usually wins. I just can't control myself for too long. But I sure do have fun in a rematch.

Kevin, 36, elementary teacher

4. What is your favorite part of giving oral sex?

The look of pleasure on my girl as I am going down on her. She gets into the mood quicker when I use my tongue on her.

James, 28, hotel clerk

I like to feel my lover's penis hit the back of my throat. I like the force of his thrusts, and maybe the fact that he could kill me with his erection if he gets carried away.

Russel, 22, drummer

I like the first taste of her musky juice. The initial slurp into her vagina always makes me hard. I taste her flavor and my brain sends an urgent erection notice to my penis.

Benny, 35, radiator rebuilder

5. What is your favorite part of getting oral sex?

When I can no longer hold back my ejaculate and I gush a stream of sperm down my lover's throat. As long as she doesn't gag, we are both happy. And even if she does gag, at least one of us is satisfied.

Reggie, 39, pharmacist

My wife finally learned how to deep throat after a year of trying. If the angle is right, she can bury my dick all the way down her throat and use my pubic hair as a mustache. As long as I keep my thrusts steady, she can time her breathing and make me climax without choking. The friction she generates along the entire length of my shaft is the best feeling on earth.

Wayne, 25, salesman

The best part of receiving oral is when I absolutely cannot hold it anymore. She keeps me on the verge for a few more minutes and then swallows every drop. The final explosion is so much more intense when she holds me back.

Russell, 32, Peace Corps

6. Do you like to have your mouth on your partner's vagina when she is climaxing?

If I am performing oral on her, then my answer is yes. I feel that when I am doing oral on her, then I should finish her in my mouth. She does the same for me. I like the way she squirms and squeals with her orgasms. She has the actions of a child given a special treat at the precise moment of climax.

Todd, 42, accounts manager

She has a weak bladder and pees all in my mouth when she climaxes. I have to be in the right mood to keep my mouth down there when I feel her tense up. Sometimes I am. More times I'm not.

Bud, 54, carpenter

When she climaxes, my mouth is on her mouth and my penis is deep inside her vagina. My mouth is nowhere near that part of the action.

Eldon, 39, state trooper

7. Is it important to you that your mate swallow?

When I was younger, making sure she swallowed was the most important thing of all. I told her that it proved her love. Now it doesn't really seem so important. I'd just as soon squirt in her hair or face or wherever. It's funny how things change over the years. Maybe I just miss the challenge of getting her to do it.

William, 35, property manager

If she wants me to swallow her love puddles, she had better be willing to drink my cum.

Joey, 20, clerk

I like the fact that my wife swallows, but I wouldn't get mad if she didn't. I know women that will not even perform oral on their men much less swallow.

Freddy, 19, busboy

8. Do you swallow?

In a simple word, yes. I love oral, so of course I swallow, but only with women.

Teddy, 27, radio jock

I drink my love's honey every chance I get. After thirty-five years of marriage, I probably don't want to know how many gallons I've swallowed. All I know is I eagerly await each tasty mouthful she gives me.

Ned, 58, doorman

Gag, puke, wretch. Swallowing is strictly a woman thing to give a man pleasure.

Beau, 21, lawn specialist

10 Orgasm

1. ***Do you experience multiple orgasms? How often? Always?***
2. ***How long do you have to wait to have sex again? A few minutes, hours?***
3. ***How long does it take your partner to climax?***
4. ***Do you ever have trouble bringing your mate to orgasm?***
5. ***Are you happy with the average time it takes women to have an orgasm compared to the time it takes men?***
6. ***Do you ever have trouble with premature ejaculation? If so, how do you handle it and how does your mate react to it?***
7. ***How often does your mate climax?***
8. ***Have you ever felt as if your lover was faking her orgasms? If so, how did you react? Did you talk about it with her?***
9. ***How do you really know your lover is satisfied with your lovemaking?***
10. ***Would she tell you if she wasn't satisfied?***

1. Do you experience multiple orgasms? How often? Always?

When I was younger, I could climax five or six times during a session of love. Now I'm lucky to get it up, much less come more than once.

Dan, 53, construction foreman

If I'm horny, I can climax three times in about ten minutes. I can feel the fluid flowing through my body like a coffeepot ready to boil. It is a powerful feeling, and I love it. When I'm charged up, I don't even lose my erection when I come. I numb out a little, take two or three more strokes, and bang—I'm good for another round of pumping.

Perry, 25, lawn specialist

Only if I am superhorny and my first climax is quick. Usually I'm a onetimer.

Doug, 29, manager, fast food

I can only climax once a night, but, boy, when I come in you, you know it. My girlfriend calls me Mr. Puddles.

Mathew, 43, jewelry maker

2. How long do you have to wait to have sex again? A few minutes, hours?

It all depends on how fast and hard the first time is. If it was slow and easy, then just a few minutes; if it was hard and fast, then a couple of hours. If I'm tired, it's the next day or night.

Gregory, 41, grease mechanic

I don't wait between orgasms. I just pump my load out the ole love pipe and go on to round two. I don't go soft. I usually don't even miss a stroke.

Wayne, 20, lumber mill operator

3. How long does it take your partner to climax?

The time it takes my wife to come is directly related to the amount of hassle she had during the day. If work was hard or the children were impossible or the bills are piling up, her climaxes take much longer. I wish we were both teenagers and able to just fuck and enjoy it. Foreplay used to consist of simply calling my baby up on the phone and telling her I was going to take her for a ride around town. She'd meet me at the door with wet panties and a big kiss. Now if the rent check is a few days late, I can fuck her forever and lick her for hours, and she still can't climax.

Chuck, 31, appliance salesman

If I take the time to give her a few minutes of foreplay, she can usually climax in about ten minutes. If I just slam my way in, it can take weeks for her to get off, and months for her to get over my piggy behavior.

Paul, 40, golf instructor

Most of the time she can climax with only a little bit of persuasion. There are times when she is not ready for me to enter her, then it takes a lot of coaxing on my part. I enjoy the ride so I don't complain.

Gary, 33, grocery clerk

4. Do you ever have trouble bringing your mate to orgasm?

Any honest man will have to say that he has had trouble bringing a girl to a climax at one time or another.

Bobby, 28, gas station attendant

No. I always take the time to make sure she has an orgasm every time. Just call me Mr. Sensitive.

Joel, 39, cabinet finisher

I have the opposite problem. My baby comes so fast, I barely have time to get inside her before she's done. She gets supersensitive after she climaxes and has to push me out of her vagina. I usually wind up jerking off on her belly.

Oliver, 24, security guard

5. Are you happy with the average time it takes women to have an orgasm compared to the time it takes men?

Maybe that is one of the many reasons why older men date younger women. A young lady is excited and ready to come much, much quicker than an older woman. It sometimes feels like climaxing is the last thing on some middle-aged women's minds. They'd rather complain about positions, ask for more foreplay, and criticize your performance. A young girl just wants to fuck and enjoy herself.

Butch, 40, marketing specialist

My wife never climaxes, so the question doesn't apply.

Carl, 28, jewelry salesman

I make it my job to take care of my needs when I have sex. I do whatever it takes to make me feel good. If my girlfriend concentrates on her own pleasure, then we usually have mutual orgasms. When she waits for me to do the job for her, she is always frustrated.

Pat, 46, operations director

I am reasonably happy with my sex life. Sometimes it takes me a while longer to come, so I don't mind its taking her a little while longer to climax at times. It doesn't matter what the reason for the delay is.

Jared, 37, land surveyor

6. Do you ever have trouble with premature ejaculation? If so, how do you handle it and how does your mate react to it?

The only time I have premature ejaculation is when I haven't had sex in a while and my girlfriend has me so turned on that I can't hold back when I do get it from her. It is not too often that this happens. When it does, she doesn't get mad because I always take care of her one way or another.

Christopher, 29, auto body repair

Sex with my wife has become so routine, I'd actually love to suffer from premature ejaculation. At least I'd be finished quicker and able to go to sleep at a decent hour.

Dean, 43, stockbroker

My girlfriend knows that I tend to come before most people, so she just starts our lovemaking with a quick suck-off. I give her a mouthful, she swallows, and then we get down to the business of fucking each other. I get the best of both worlds. I'm a lucky little quick spurt.

Raymond, 23, singer

7. How often does your mate climax?

My wife climaxes whenever she gets serious about sex or is short on time. If she concentrates, she has an orgasm. If we have to be somewhere in an hour and I grab a quickie, she can come like a bunny rabbit. Or maybe she is just a great actress.

Chris, 26, florist

My lover climaxes more often than most women sneeze. She just squeezes her thighs tight around my thrusting penis, closes her eyes, breathes short, little, rapid gasps, and has an orgasm. She can do it about eight times before she falls asleep, totally exhausted. I used to think she was faking it, but five years of weekly orgasms is a long time to fake something.

Horace, 46, government worker

My mate is one of those women who can usually climax only once if we have been at it for a while. If it was a quickie, then she can come again shortly.

Ronny, 37, route salesman

8. Have you ever felt as if your lover was faking her orgasms? If so, how did you react? Did you talk about it with her?

If I felt she was faking it, then we don't have the relationship I thought we did. I want her to be comfortable with me enough to say, "Hey, it was not that good for me," and tell me why. That way I could try to correct it so that it will not happen again. That is how a true relationship should be.

Tim, 45, truck driver

I knew she was faking it. She knew I knew she was faking it. Even then she kept on faking it for months. I didn't really see the point of her theatrics, but I liked the way she wiggled and clamped down on my penis. I guess I was just too selfish to call her bluff.

Dana, 36, flea market merchant

I once questioned a woman about the sincerity of her screaming orgasms. She got mad and refused to fuck me anymore. Now a woman can be quoting Shakespeare and blow off a Roman candle in bed and I will never question her. I've learned my lesson.

Art, 43, antique dealer

9. How do you really know your lover is satisfied with your lovemaking?

Because my girlfriend is drop-dead beautiful and if she wasn't happy with our love life, she would get a new one. Guys are constantly coming on to her everywhere she goes, and she always comes home to me. It sure ain't because I'm rich.

Scott, 25, auto mechanic

I know my baby is satisfied with our sex life because if she wasn't, I'd know it in about one second. She speaks her mind about everything from favorite brands of soda to which TV show to watch. So you know she is going to voice her demands in bed. Anyone who gets worked up over plastic grocery bags isn't afraid to tell me how to lick her pussy.

Bud, 42, land developer

That's a tough question. I believe she is satisfied with our sex life, but who knows what really goes on in a woman's head.

She tells me it is great, so until I know different, I have to believe her and her love for me.

George, 32, store owner

10. Would she tell you if she wasn't satisfied?

You bet she would, just like I would let her know if I wasn't satisfied. We would try to work it out. If not, we'd go our separate ways.

Joel, 24, store clerk

My girlfriend would only tell me something was wrong as she threw the keys in my face and stormed out of my life. That is part of our present problem. She is so concerned with appearances and what everyone thinks that I doubt if she has any real feelings of her own anymore.

Nolan, 40, car dealer

She wouldn't tell me shit. She'd have the maid tell my driver that something was wrong in the bedroom. The whole domestic staff would know all about the most intimate details of my sex life before I heard a thing. I'm always the last to know anything, and I pay all the bills.

Sam, 46, record producer

11 Before & After Sex

1. ***Can you have great sex without foreplay?***
2. ***What is perfect foreplay?***
3. ***How long should foreplay last?***
4. ***Should men be as focused on foreplay toward women as women toward men?***
5. ***What type of foreplay drives you wild?***
6. ***What type of foreplay drives your partner wild?***
7. ***How do you feel after sex—turned on, sleepy, hungry, refreshed?***
8. ***What do you like to do after sex?***
9. ***What does your lover like to do after sex?***

1. Can you have great sex without foreplay?

I'm a guy. Who needs foreplay?

Brian, 19, student

Sometimes life itself is foreplay. After a day of just being together, shopping at the mall, singing songs on the car ride home, my wife walks into the living room horny and ready. I don't have to do anything more than hike her dress up and do her on the sofa. I'm a lucky guy.

Willie, 30, inventory specialist

I would be lying if I said I needed foreplay. My wife has to have some kind of foreplay for great sex. I wish she would be able to do a quickie every now and then.

Tony, 31, teller

2. What is perfect foreplay?

To me perfect foreplay is when both partners are ready and can't wait to have sex.

Brad, 18, student

Perfect foreplay is when my new wife is waiting for me on the eighteenth hole at the club, wearing her little white tennis skirt with no panties on underneath.

Sidney, 40, commercial real estate developer

I love it when my girlfriend throws her books on the floor, takes me by the hand, and lays me on the living room floor to make love. She unzips my pants with her teeth while squeezing my nipples between her fingers. By the time she has my penis in her mouth, I'm ready to roll her over and fuck the stars out of her.

Jamie, 20, college student

3. How long should foreplay last?

Long enough to get my girlfriend aroused, but not long enough to make my tongue sore.

Matt, 20, fast-food worker

Foreplay should last long enough to make her ready, but not so long that she loses interest. Too many appetizers can ruin the main course. I want the gravy and the meat!

Clarence, 48, produce seller

Long enough to arouse all the senses of both people.

Johnny, 24, data clerk

I think foreplay should last for the least amount of time possible for two lovers to be ready to explode.

Ken, 35, lawyer

4. Should men be as focused on foreplay toward women as women toward men?

Yes, a female needs the extra attention so she will be wet enough that I can enjoy her and not hurt like hell from her being too dry. Yes, I'm a prick. I know it, and I'm proud.

Shawn, 21, bartender

I think men should be more aware of foreplay because women simply need more foreplay to enjoy sex. A man who isn't willing to make his woman feel good doesn't deserve her affection. I want my wife to feel loved, honored, and special. I want her to be happy enough with my sexual attention that she doesn't even think about another man.

Roger, 47, chemical engineer

If the relationship is hot enough, the only foreplay a man needs to give a woman is a kiss and a quick jerk on the zipper of her jeans.

Neal, 19, motocross racer

5. What type of foreplay drives you wild?
I like the seduction. I like the flirting and teasing and provocative gestures. The sizzle of anticipation is sometimes better than the taste of reality.

Ed, 34, college professor

I like it when my girlfriend puts her hot little tongue in my ear and tickles me. I laugh and get an erection that almost hurts.

Bo, 39, newsletter publisher

When my wife flashes me in public, I lose all reason and feel like a schoolboy again. I go dick stupid. It's a wonder I haven't been arrested for public stupidity.

Mark, 51, barber

When a woman lets me know that she wants me just as bad as I want her. I don't like it when I have to do all the pursuing. I like a woman who is not afraid to show me what she wants.

Joel, 36, bus driver

6. What type of foreplay drives your partner wild?
Slow, sensual foreplay, taking-my-time foreplay, make her see stars and then deep, hard screwing. Gets her every time. She is putty in my hands and mouth.

Carl, 34, roofer

My girl likes it when I dribble chocolate milk on her nipples at the beach. She knows when I head for the snack bar, it's time for her juices to start flowing.

Bruce, 20, lifeguard

My wife goes crazy when I hum on her clitoris. She doesn't even care what song I hum. She just loves the vibrations.

Mick, 29, bookbinder

7. How do you feel after sex—turned on, sleepy, hungry, refreshed?

I'm usually cuddly, snugly, and almost pathetic. After I bare my soul, expose my naked lust, and share the primal screams of passion, I'm ready to suck my thumb and sleep like a baby.

Troy, 24, medical student

Like most guys I feel like I want to run out into the street and disappear.

Jason, 33, body-shop repairman

I feel like I can face another day of disappointments, rejection, and injustice.

Samuel, 37, schoolteacher

After sex I am dying of thirst and in bad need of a cigarette. When that's taken care of, I can relax with my baby in my arms and drift off to sleep. If it's in the daytime, then I can leap tall buildings in a couple of bounds. I am ready to slay dragons.

Leroy, 33, dental assistant

8. What do you like to do after sex?

It depends on the time of day. I like to drift off to sleep if it's late at night. If it's in the morning or during the day, perhaps after a quickie, I am ready to take on the world.

Corey, 23, waiter

I like to eat chocolate-covered peanuts. My girlfriend keeps a big glass jar full of them by the bed. Sometimes I will rush through the sex just to get the candy. It depends on how hungry I am, and how bitchy she has been to me that day.

Bo, 20, salesman

I like to cuddle and spoon and just melt into each other. I'm a real baby after I get my rocks off.

Rodney, 33, insurance claims manager

9. What does your lover like to do after sex?

My lover likes to talk, and talk; about our relationship, about sex, about her friends' relationships, about her friends' sex lives. Sometimes I just want to stuff her panties in her mouth to shut her up.

Luke, 28, civil engineer

She likes to count the change I leave on the table. It's a joke. I'm kidding.

Bobby, 35, financial writer

John likes to hold me in his arms and tell me how great our love is. He holds me firmly and confidently, and we fall asleep satisfied and a little sore.

Robert, 30, restaurant manager

My lover likes for us to lie wrapped up in each other's arms and just chill out.

Charles, 29, insurance sales

12 Sex Talk

1. ***Do you like to talk dirty?***
2. ***What do you say when you are talking dirty?***
3. ***Do you like for your mate to talk dirty?***
4. ***What does your mate say to make you hot?***
5. ***Do you make noise during sex?***
6. ***Do you like for your mate to make noise during sex?***
7. ***Are you a screamer?***

1. Do you like to talk dirty?

I am currently dating a lady who really can't stand dirty language. I'm used to girls who get off on raunchy love chat, but Sharon is simply appalled by the whole idea. The first time we had sex, I was getting ready to climax and I told her that I was going to fuck the shit out of her. She slapped my face and started crying. I felt like a complete jerk.

Randy, 22, disc jockey

I talk so foul at work, by the time I get home, I'm all cussed out. I like to be quiet and submissive and let my wife do all the dirty talk and work.

Burt, 33, traffic cop

I only talk dirty with women after I get to know them. Some women act so completely freaked out by nasty language that it completely ruins a relationship. I usually bite my tongue until I feel real safe in bed with a lady, or until she tells me to "ram the shit out of my pussy with your hair rod." That's usually a good sign.

Steve, 29, bouncer

Typically I don't talk dirty, though there are times during heavy sex that we both talk very dirty. It seems to make her hotter.

Jeremy, 36, teacher

2. What do you say when you are talking dirty?

I will tell my wife exactly what I'm going to do to her. I tell her that I'm going to lick her like an ice cream cone and that she is going to get my Popsicle stuck deep inside her honey box. Is that dirty or not? That's the way I talk to her.

Kevin, 24, computer programmer

I talk rude, crude, and forceful. My girl knows it's a big game, and she gets into playing the role. The people next door probably think we are a bunch of grunting pigs. Well, I say fuck them.

Byron, 27, driving instructor

3. Do you like for your mate to talk dirty?

The first time my girlfriend talked dirty during sex, it scared me. We didn't really know each other all that well, and during my more athletic moves she started giving me very direct and verbal instructions about what she wanted me to do to her.

Once I got used to the idea of hearing the new love of my life pleading with me to fuck her until it made her cry, everything was fine. I still can't believe her cute little mouth can say such nasty things.

Perry, 28, social worker

Because it is so unlike my petite, little, perfect wife, I love it when she talks like a longshoreman. Hearing such nasty things coming out of her sweet, moist lips makes me hard. It is the contradiction that makes it so appealing.

Jackson, 40, telecommunications developer

My wife will not talk dirty; she says it is too degrading. She thinks only trash mouths talk like that.

William, 63, semiretired

4. What does your mate say to make you hot?

My lover tells me in very exact details what he wants me to do to him. How deep he wants it. How he likes for me to perform oral on him, etc. I eat him up when he talks like that. It makes me hot to trot.

Teddy, 36, ladies' garment sales

My baby whispers. She can be reading the phone book in her whispery "fuck me" voice, and I'll get an erection. She speaks softly and I carry my big stick to her every time.

Craig, 35, state historian research assistant

She tells me that she loves me.

Patrick, 27, inventory auditor

5. Do you make noise during sex?

I grunt like a pig. I like being loud and physical. I become a caveman. I regress to my most primitive form. I don't recite poetry. I don't pose philosophical questions. I just make guttural sounds and enjoy the hell out of what I'm doing.

Lou, 33, asphalt worker

My wife and I have gained so much weight after ten years of being couch potatoes that the only sound we make during sex is the noise of fat slapping against fat.

Ralph, 45, office manager

I like to shout when I climax. Sometimes my wife stuffs my underwear in my mouth to keep the kids from waking up.

Herman, 29, tool and die worker

I am quiet when I make love to my girlfriend. I look her straight in the eyes. I get into the pleasures we are both feeling. I like the intensity that is on her face as we are doing it. There were times when she tried to talk to me during sex, but it just broke the momentum. Then it takes a while to get back into the rhythm.

Jake, 37, pharmacist

6. Do you like for your mate to make noise during sex?

Absolutely, how else will I know that she is enjoying it? Some women fake it so well.

Ken, 25, sound operator

As long as she doesn't fart or belch during sex, she can make any noise she likes.

Alan, 50, tow motor operator

7. Are you a screamer?

Hell, yes, I'm a screamer.

Jack, 24, sailor

I like to voice my approval, so I yell when I feel good.

Barry, 40, stockbroker

I become so focused on my orgasm that I sometimes forget to breathe. I gasp, but I don't scream.

Sammy, 20, student

I only scream when I'm scared, and being in bed with a woman is not scary. Besides, I'm particular who I go to bed with these days.

Rick, 45, pawn-store owner

13 Sex Toys

1. ***Have you ever used sex toys?***
2. ***Describe some of your sex toys and your experiences with them.***
3. ***Do you use lotions?***
4. ***Do you use creams and edible playthings?***
5. ***What is the craziest or wildest sex toy you have ever heard about?***
6. ***What is the wildest sex toy you have ever used?***
7. ***Have you ever had a bad experience with a sex toy?***

1. Have you ever used sex toys?

If a woman needs a toy in bed with her, she's not the right woman for me. I have enough games going on in my life without bringing play toys into my sex life.

Harry, 45, carpet layer

I like to play in bed with dolls, toys, and the stuff you find in the bottom of a kid's playroom closet. You can have a great time with a plastic Slinky, a bottle of bubbles, and a naked babe.

Jesse, 19, food mart cashier

We like to play with *Star Wars* action figures in bed. My girlfriend likes to get real friendly with the little furry animal people and the weird aliens. I think we lost a few during our last session.

Tony, 23, camera salesman

My girlfriend likes for me to use toys on her, but she will never use them on me. That doesn't seem fair to me. Maybe I'll try one on a day when she's not home.

Jordan, 36, furniture sales

2. Describe some of your sex toys and your experiences with them.

I don't have any sex toys. We do use some unusual household items from time to time. For instance, my girlfriend has used a douche-bottle tip anally. She has used tapered candles, the cordless-phone antenna, etc. I think her favorite item is my African statue that is about nine inches tall.

Daniel, 27, sales rep

I have used rubber snakes, rubber chickens, even a pile of fake rubber dog poop in bed before. I like to keep things a little crazy. My wife is used to me after all these years. It keeps getting harder and harder to surprise her, though the wind-up plastic penis did give her a chuckle last week.

Bernie, 27, souvenir salesman

3. Do you use lotions?

I used to use love lotions in bed until I discovered that they dissolved my hairpiece. I went through two thousand dollars' worth of fake hair in six months before they figured out the cherry-flavored climax-prolong jelly was melting my synthetic hair.

George, 48, accountant

Spit and sweat are all I need, and I've got gallons of both.

Karl, 26, roadwork

I like to use baby shampoo on my bottom when my girlfriend and I play in the bathtub. She takes a handful of the shampoo and inserts it up my anus. I hold it in as long as possible, and then I blow it out. Sometimes rainbow-colored bubbles pop out, and we laugh ourselves silly. We call it our weird but cheap entertainment.

Raymond, 29, civil servant

We don't use anything that comes in a bottle, but we use all natural products. We are nature buffs.

Jamie, 27, sports jockey

4. Do you use creams and edible playthings?

My girlfriend and I have tried several of the edible products on the market. We don't like them because they usually taste rather bland, and neither one of us likes the creams that we have tried. Give me a bottle of wine, cheese, crackers, grapes, and food to play with and we can go all night.

Jody, 21, student

I like to suck eggnog out of my baby's pussy during the holidays. She just has to remember to douche after we get finished or she gets a horrible infection all through January.

Dave, 32, road crew manager

I like to take a chocolate-covered cherry and insert it up my wife's vagina. I suck it out of her pussy, and she gets the greatest rush. As long as it doesn't get smashed up inside her and start leaking, we never have any problems. I love taking her new cherry and biting down really hard on it, as long as there aren't any little hairs sticking in it.

Curtis, 48, factory worker

5. What is the craziest or wildest sex toy you have ever heard about?

A plastic Godzilla with a spine of tingling ridges is my girlfriend's favorite object of love.

Gary, 21, stockboy

My girlfriend loves her good-luck rabbit-foot keychain. She rubs it, loves it, and keeps a long string tied to the chain in case she gets a little too wild.

Pete, 29, computer artist

I guess I'm still wet behind the ears. I've never tried or heard of any unusual sex toys. Maybe I'll hear or find out about some soon.

Randy, 23, computer student

6. What is the wildest sex toy you have ever used?

A three-headed dildo. We inserted two of the heads into her and one into my anus. We had the most amazing sex. I firmly believe that three heads are actually better than two.

Gordan, 29, graphic artist

My girlfriend likes it when I put toy soldiers in her pussy. Who am I to judge? I'm kinda fond of the missile launcher myself.

Gil, 23, cook

7. Have you ever had a bad experience with a sex toy?

I once dated a girl strictly for sex. Since I didn't love her, or even really like her very much, I guess she was my sex toy and nothing else. Because the relationship wasn't really based on anything other than sex, it ended badly. She remains very bitter toward me and my family.

Joey, 29, fisherman

I got shocked by an anal vibrator once. It was only battery powered, so I wasn't in any real danger, but it did scare me.

Jan, 41, real estate appraiser

I've never gotten up the nerve to try a sex toy much less have a bad experience with one. Maybe I'll try one tonight to see what all the fuss is about.

Kyle, 19, graduate student

14 Erotic Films & Photographs

1. ***Do you like to read pornographic magazines?***
2. ***Do pictures of naked women turn you on?***
3. ***Do pictures of naked men turn you on?***
4. ***Do you like to read erotic literature?***
5. ***Have you ever posed nude?***
6. ***Would you pose nude? Under what circumstances?***
7. ***Have you ever watched hard-core movies by yourself? With your mate, the guys, anyone? Did you enjoy them?***
8. ***Would you like to star in a pornographic film?***
9. ***Have you ever made a sexual home video?***
10. ***Has your mate ever given you nude photos or a sexual video of herself for a surprise gift?***

1. Do you like to read pornographic magazines?

You mean they have words in those things?

Paul, 25, bank teller

When I was young, I craved porno. Now I'd rather spend time with a real woman. Besides, the beach is filled with women who look like they belong in magazines, and I get to talk to them in person.

Zak, 20, surf-shop salesman

No, I don't read the articles. I just look at the babes. Maybe I'll start reading the articles when my libido starts slowing down. Right now I get too hot looking at the pictures to stop and read anything. I keep losing my place and read the same sentence over and over.

Rob, 20, waiter

2. Do pictures of naked women turn you on?

Do bears shit in the woods? Seriously though, yes, pictures are a type of turn-on, but I'd rather see the real thing before my eyes. Like the cola ad says, "Ain't nothin' like the real thing, baby."

Lou, 26, technician

I spent my entire high school years surrounded by hundreds of pictures of naked girls. They were the last thing I saw before I went to sleep, and the first thing I saw every morning, and I spent all night fucking their brains out in my dreams. Reality sucks. Now I have a roommate and I can't get away with such childish shit.

Jonathon, 20, college student

3. Do pictures of naked men turn you on?

I'm not gay. I don't even think about nude guys, much less look at pictures of them. When I go to the public rest room, I look straight ahead and read the writing on the wall. And if

I ever see my own phone number staring back at me, someone is going to get the crap beat out of him.

Eugene, 20, military policeman

I look at photos of naked men to see how their penises compare to mine. I figure if their penises are impressive enough to earn them money, I want to see how I measure up. As far as I can tell, I've got nothing to be ashamed of. I'd put my penis up next to theirs anytime. That sounds kinda queer, doesn't it?

Kenny, 25, motorcycle mechanic

Nude male pictures do not turn me on. I do look at them sometimes to see if I measure up to the standards the books use for sexy men. For the record, I don't.

Billy, 33, factory worker

4. Do you like to read erotic literature?

I read anything I can get my hands on. I love to read. Maybe that's why I became an editor. I have read every day of my life since I picked up my first book at about age six.

Brian, 43, magazine editor

Sometimes words make me harder than pictures. I like to let my mind paint the picture the words give me. I especially enjoy the stories about spanking naughty women wearing those tight leather skirts.

Rory, 35, meatpacker

I like to read trashy sex novels written by people with initials for their first names. The rougher, the better. It gives me a break from the day-to-day routine. Instead of being the security cop of a warehouse of auto supplies, I become the personal love slave of a French princess in the time of powdered wigs and lace panties.

Johnny, 29, security officer

5. Have you ever posed nude?

My girlfriend recently talked me into letting her take a picture of my erection for a photo art class. She had me lie down in the middle of a still life of vegetables and raw meat. If you look real close at the poster, you can see my boner right next to the pig's feet and the chicken livers. She calls it art. I call it weird.

Stan, 20, engineering student

I can still feel the intense embarrassment I went through every time my mother dug out the old photo album and showed my latest girlfriend the totally humiliating picture of me butt naked in the bathtub when I was three years old. I haven't appeared nude in any pictures since, and this one still haunts me.

Ronald, 35, electrician

When I was younger, I posed for a guy who loved to take nude pictures of guys with boners. I just sat on a barstool and smiled in my birthday suit. He didn't touch me, and I made twenty-five bucks. I guess those pictures are floating around the Internet somewhere right this second. If I did it again, I'd charge more.

Darien, 22, swimming instructor

I have never and will never pose nude. Some things are meant to be kept private and to your self. I don't have any qualms about nudity. I just don't want to pose nude.

Jay, 26, salesclerk

6. Would you pose nude? Under what circumstances?

I would pose nude under any circumstances. I am an exhibitionist at heart. Besides, I have a good-looking body.

Joshua, 23, teacher's aide

If they would retouch my pecker and make it about six inches longer and two inches thicker, I'd do it in a heartbeat. Hell, I'd probably put it on a business card and meet a whole new class of people.

Andy, 30, office furniture salesman

I would pose nude with my girlfriend if she stood in front of me and all you could see of me was my face smiling and my hands grabbing her tits.

Forrest, 26, construction worker

If anybody is willing to see my naked, wrinkled pecker, I'll pay them to look at it!

James, 50, dentist

7. Have you ever watched hard-core movies by yourself? With your mate, the guys, anyone? Did you enjoy them?

I have a collection of about eighty porno tapes. I have a little bit of everything from fantasy to lesbian to interracial to amateur to light bondage. I like to get a new one every couple of weeks and watch it in the privacy of my apartment. My girlfriend doesn't know about my collection, and the idea of watching it with other guys is really gross and repulsive to me. I'm not gay or bisexual, and even though I have seen hundreds of naked guys ejaculate on video, I've seen even more women have explicit sex. I'm not sure why I like porno. Maybe I just like to see all those different healthy, willing bodies and faces having really energetic sex. I don't have any other hobbies.

Barry, 27, nurse

I like to watch pornos in the privacy of my home, where I can relax and take care of business. I've tried to watch a few with my girlfriend, but it makes me too nervous. I'm afraid she will think I'm a pervert if I enjoy them too much. Some things are better done alone behind locked doors.

Don, 31, housepainter

Yes, I've watched hard-core pornos, but not by myself. My girlfriend and I like to watch a flick occasionally. Only we don't ever make it to the end of the tape. We always end up screwing right there on the living room floor. I have never watched them with guys though. Maybe if I were at a stag party.

Guy, 32, steelworker

8. Would you like to star in a pornographic film?

Maybe so, if it was done tastefully. What red-blooded male would not like to strut his stuff in front of a camera with a gorgeous babe?

Roger, 27, struggling artist

The only way they'd let me star in a porno flick was if I sold my house to finance the entire film. And since I would be the only person in the world who would want to see a porno picture with me in the lead role, I would lose my money, my house, and my ass. Thanks, but no thanks.

Elmer, 50, department store manager

If I got to choose the women and the positions, I'd probably do it. From what I hear, the women have all the power in those pictures. The guys lose their erections. The women smell bad and don't even brush their teeth. The women make twice as much money and can fake their whole performances. They make jokes about their male coworkers and really just want to be lesbians anyway. Isn't that what you hear?

Harlan, 31, housepainter

9. Have you ever made a sexual home video?

Every year since the first Betamax recorder and home video cameras were sold to the public, my wife and I have made sexy tapes of our lovemaking. We started out with grainy black-and-white tapes, graduated to high-quality color productions with special effects and computer-generated edits and titles. The new digital video cameras are next on our wish list. We love technology and sex. Maybe someday you'll be able to see twenty years of our collected works on the World Wide Web.

Daryl, 48, chemist

I caught my ex-girlfriend cheating on me with her girlfriend by accident. I had planned on seeing her masturbate or play with her vibrator when I originally hid my camcorder on the bookshelf. Instead I caught her having totally disgusting sex with Amanda, the next-door neighbor. I used to think I would be turned on seeing two women together. I was wrong, especially when one of them is supposed to be in love with me.

Rodney, 21, fast-food worker

I haven't had the opportunity to make a video while having sex. Give me a few years and I'm sure I will be on the big screen.

Roy, 19, unemployed

10. Has your mate ever given you nude photos or a sexual video of herself for a surprise gift?

I am a professional photographer so I have taken lots of nude pictures of my girlfriend. The only problem is, after I have them developed, she takes them and hides them. She says it is to protect herself in case we split up. She doesn't want anyone else to get them. I tell her she is crazy because she is really gorgeous and has a body to match. Maybe one day she will trust me.

Bill, 38, journal photographer

I loved the sexy photos my wife gave me of herself in a see-through nightie, until I stopped to think about who took the pictures. She says it was a female photographer, and that she had a great time. Is that supposed to make me feel better?

Preston, 30, dry cleaner

My girlfriend secretly videotaped us having sex last week. People sure look stupid when they fuck, don't you think? I never knew my butt was so hairy.

Vance, 44, truck driver

15 Strip Clubs

1. **_Have you ever been to a strip club?_**
2. **_Does your mate frequent strip clubs? If yes, does it bother you?_**
3. **_Have you ever worked in a strip club?_**
4. **_Would you consider working in a strip club?_**
5. **_Do you think all strip club dancers are prostitutes?_**
6. **_Should prostitution be legalized?_**
7. **_Do strip clubs turn you on?_**

1. Have you ever been to a strip club?

I have spent hundreds of hours and thousands of dollars in strip clubs and topless bars over the years. And you know what? It still cost me about a tenth of what I've had to pay in alimony for my two-year marriage to a calculating gold digger. At least the strippers were nice to me.

Dave, 46, retired military

I make it a point to visit strip clubs every time I go anywhere. I've been to the best and the worst, and I've had a great time every time. Some people like to sample the native foods when they travel. I like to see, and sometimes touch, the local pussy.

Harold, 36, salesman

No, I haven't been to a strip club. In my town you have to be twenty-one. I can't wait to come of age and see what all the fanfare is about.

Benjamin, 20, student

2. Does your mate frequent strip clubs? If yes, does it bother you?

My wife went to see some male strippers with the girls from work, and I'm still recovering from it. She came home so hot and horny, she literally attacked me in the den. It was great! I don't care if she was thinking of her little stripping studs while we made love, the fact remains that it was my penis that exploded twice. Her fantasy climax was made possible by my real ejaculation. I was dreaming about my own little cheerleader anyway.

Raymond, 32, bail bondsman

My girlfriend is a hairdresser and she has several friends who are female strippers. She does their hair and then goes to see how her work holds up on the stage. She calls it research, but if I did it, she'd call it bullshit.

Andy, 24, hairstylist

My mate does not have the nerve to watch me undress much less see a bunch of guys strip before her eyes. Maybe she will loosen up with age. In the meantime, I won't push her to go see them.

Linden, 23, hotel clerk

3. Have you ever worked in a strip club?

No, I haven't, but that's not to say that I wouldn't if I needed the money. I have a nice healthy body and I love to dance.

Patrick, 20, college student

I was a bartender at a topless bar in Florida. I saw naked women all day. Big deal! After the first hundred or so tits, they all start looking the same. The girls wanted to cry on my shoulder, borrow my car, and spend my money. They were having some kind of emotional meltdown every other day. I really believe your average secretary next door has a better sex life than the working girls.

Carlton, 35, bartender

4. Would you consider working in a strip club?

I think working in a strip club as a bartender or bouncer would be horrible. It would make the forbidden pleasure of seeing women naked into something mundane. It would become just another job. I don't want to see the raw underbelly of the illusion. I don't want to get to know the girls in the bright sunlight or learn about their problems. When I watch a woman strip and play with herself onstage, I don't even want to consider that she has a kid at home with the flu. I don't want to know that Fatima, the Amazing Sex Toy, is really Cindy from Toledo.

Jim, 23, graduate student

I danced nude for a couple of weeks when I was between jobs. It was strange for about ten minutes, then it didn't really seem like a big deal. Old guys just sat at the edge of the stage and started up at my balls. A couple of guys tried to grab me, but the bouncers always kept them away. I wasn't gay, so I didn't make extra money doing "private" sessions. Most of the other dancers would do anything the customers asked for. I only lasted a couple of weeks. Maybe if I had been dancing for horny women, it might have been better.

Kenny, 20, factory worker

I don't think I could actually work in a strip club. I have been a bartender before, but there's a different atmosphere in a strip club. A lot of sleazy women work in those clubs. Not all, but most of them are slut-puppies.

Jeff, 31, ex-bartender

5. Do you think all strip club dancers are prostitutes?

The only strippers I've met that I'd consider prostitutes were the ones with a drug problem. An attractive girl can make as much as five hundred dollars a night just by dancing. She doesn't *need* to have sex with strangers when she's making three thousand dollars a week. But if she likes cocaine or crack, that is an entirely different story. Then she will do anything with anybody and still not have enough cash to keep her satisfied. I've seen it happen a dozen times.

Buddy, 35, nightclub security guard

Strippers are either young, single mothers with lots of bills to pay, or drug addicts with expensive habits. I have yet to meet one who is trying to work her way through law school. That only happens in movies.

Brian, 27, mobile disc jockey

Some of the sweetest women I've ever known were professional strippers. They look good, they have money, and if they get to know you as a regular person, they can be your best friend.

Pat, 30, beverage distributor

The only strip club I've ever been in, all the girls were very loose and would leave with anyone who would pay them.

Frank, 32, policeman

6. Should prostitution be legalized?

I really could care less if it's legalized or not. It is a profession as old as time. Nowadays if a prostitute is arrested, she is right back on the street even before the police are done writing the report.

Byran, 34, research assistant

I firmly believe they should legalize it. Then the prostitutes could pay their fair share of income taxes. We work and pay taxes. Why shouldn't they?

Wynn, 26, video store manager

I think a huge number of marriages would qualify as legal prostitution if the law was changed. My wife certainly makes me pay through the nose for the little bit of sex I get.

Rodney, 38, industrial-supply sales rep

7. Do strip clubs turn you on?

I think strip clubs are dirty, degrading, and a waste of money. But I still go to them every week. I like the nasty side of it. It isn't respectable. It isn't clean and packaged. I like the honky-tonk, gritty atmosphere. I like the booze, cigar smoke, and the abundance of young, female flesh, like the fallen angels with their pouty lips, firm tits, and shaven pussies.

Reggie, 30, newspaper reporter

I think strip clubs are sad. The girls are just peddling their bodies as cheap entertainment. The guys are pigs. The whole idea is degrading to both sexes.

Paul, 22, graduate student

I do not frequent strip clubs. They are tasteless and degrading to the women. They take the downtrodden girls who are having a tough time and turn them into drug addicts or whores.

Jeff, 56, broker

16 Places

1. ***Where do you like to make love?***
2. ***Where does your mate like to make love?***
3. ***Have you ever had sex in a public location? Describe.***
4. ***Name at least one public location you would like to try, but haven't, and why you haven't.***
5. ***Tell us a friend's tale of sex in a public place.***
6. ***What's the worst place you have ever made love, and why was it so bad?***
7. ***What do you think about sex outdoors? Any personal experiences?***
8. ***Have you ever had sex in the water? Swimming pool, lake, ocean?***
9. ***Automobile sex? Driving down the road or parked?***

1. Where do you like to make love?

I have spent thousands of dollars making my bedroom into what some people may consider a cliché, but I don't care. I have a round, motorized bed. I can dim the lights and control the multichannel stereo from my pillow. The ceiling is covered with mirrors, and my satin sheets are jet-black. I have a wet bar and a mini-frig at my fingertips, and I could live in this room for months if I had to. Some guys spend all their money on cars. I spend mine on something a little more personal. Though some guys may think it's stupid, chicks really love it.

Harry, 26, assistant tailor

The futon in front of the fireplace is perfect for an evening of soft, sexy lovemaking.

Terrence, 31, software developer

I make love anywhere I am at the time I'm horny. I will only draw the line in public places where I would definitely get arrested for indecent exposure. The chance of maybe getting caught is part of the thrill. My girl is a willing participant.

Gary, 24, short order cook

2. Where does your mate like to make love?

She will only have sex in the house, where the kids can't see us. Luckily the kids are always out playing in our backyard in the afternoon.

Jack, 37, real estate sales

My lover wants sex in some of the strangest places. On a ski lift. We have done it on top of the Empire State Building. Sex in a cave. The stranger the place, the better she likes it.

Bruce, 43, pharmacist

My girlfriend likes to fuck and play in historic landmark houses. Her goal is to have sex in every U.S. president's home before she dies. I figure the White House may be the toughest one to crack unless I can come up with a large enough political contribution or find a compromising video of the man in the Oval Office.

Mark, 36, park ranger

3. Have you ever had sex in a public location? Describe.

My girlfriend and I like to make love on the roof of her apartment building. There aren't any higher buildings nearby so there really isn't much danger of being seen. It just feels so great to be in the middle of thousands of people, completely naked. I know people can hear us sometimes, because they'll yell smart-ass comments. They just can't see us. As long as the building's maintenance guys don't get too curious, we'll just keep on pounding away.

Joey, 19, grocery sacker

When I was a teenager, we made love at the park in the backseat of my Ford. Most of my friends discovered the joys of sex in the same place. At any given time there would be as many as a dozen cars bouncing and creaking up and down by the swing sets. The policemen never gave us a problem. They'd just shine their spotlights on us sometimes and warn us to be careful. As far as I know, no one ever got hurt, robbed, or bothered. Now my kids can't even play in that same park in broad daylight because of all the drugs and gangs.

Sam, 45, electrical supplies salesman

Yes, we have sex in public. We live out in the country. It is very open and we take every opportunity to fuck outside while the rest of the world goes by. I remember having sex in a clearing once, and just as I was starting toward my climax, I looked up and saw this huge buck heading straight for us. I don't know if he smelled the sex or was just hungry. Just the sight of this deer coming toward me made me come with great primal force. I think maybe I was subconsciously daring it to try and stop me from getting my rocks off.

Darren, 34, landscaping owner

4. Name at least one public location you would like to try, but haven't, and why you haven't.

I would give anything to have sex on the express train. I haven't because the state I live in doesn't have passenger trains.

Joey, 26, driver education teacher

I'd like to fuck my wife in Times Square. The thought of such a public display excites me, but knowing my luck, I probably wouldn't be able to get an erection and some guy would come by and steal my wallet.

Kevin, 30, landscape artist

Making love on the security bomb detector at the airport would be worth remembering. I like the idea of just jumping on the conveyor belt and having the cops x-ray our pumping bodies as we go through the machine. It would certainly give people something to talk about while they wait for their flights.

Cliff, 19, art student

5. Tell us a friend's tale of sex in a public place.

My best friend spent the worst summer of his life working in a live sex club in New York City. He went up to the Big Apple with hopes of taking Broadway by storm. His five hundred dollars lasted about two weeks. His hometown résumé totally underwhelmed everyone, and he was freaking out. He took a job handing out discount coupons for strip bars, then discovered that he could make enough money to live on if he could have sex onstage three times a night. So he became a live sex performer for two months. He went to auditions for plays during the day and had sex onstage at night. When it came time to go back to college, he came back home and decided to switch his major to prelaw.

Tim, 20, student

My cousin was about ten years old when he let a twelve-year-old girl on the playground talk him into pulling his pecker out and showing it off. He knew he shouldn't, but that didn't stop him. Once he had his pants down around his knees, the girl pushed him down and started yelling for everybody to come look at his "dingdong." The teachers didn't find it amusing at all. People still give him grief about it, and it happened twenty-seven years ago. People in small towns never forget a thing.

Daryl, 38, mechanical engineer

I believe I have led a sheltered life. I don't know of anyone's sex habit in a private place much less a public place. Anyone out there got a story to tell me?

Ryan, 18, freshman

6. What's the worst place you have ever made love, and why was it so bad?

I once did it in a field of soybeans. Talk about rough sex. It was hard on my backside 'cause she was on top.

Brad, 23, farmer

In my parents house—while they were in the next room.

Caleb, 19, unemployed

On my computer desk. While we were screwing, the computer fell off and broke. At the time I was oblivious to the desk shaking. I didn't see the computer sliding. It cost me over three thousand dollars to replace it.

Bailey, 33, computer programmer

7. What do you think about sex outdoors? Any personal experiences?

I love sex outdoors during the summer. We have an enclosed front porch with the traditional white swing, like many Southern homes. The screens keep the bugs away and allow the breeze to circulate over our bodies. My wife makes a pitcher of lemonade and brings out a bottle of Kentucky bourbon for shooters. We light a mosquito candle out on the walkway and just snuggle up on our swing for a few relaxing hours of love and sex. We usually have a wonderful time as long as the dogs don't get a whiff of our scent and start barking their heads off.

Reid, 37, public accountant

Every time we try to make love outside in the backyard, the neighborhood dogs start barking and having a fit. It doesn't matter what time of day it is, we can't even finish a quickie. I believe they can smell the scent.

Paul, 32, store manager

I really appreciate the beauty of Mother Nature. I always find time for sex outdoors. I like to find a secluded area and be two with nature. The only drawback is the bugs and their intimate bites.

John, 34, automaker

8. Have you ever had sex in the water? Swimming pool, lake, ocean?

My wife and I take vacations every year or so to an island state in the Pacific. We both love sex in the water. There is something about sex in the water and on the beach that really keeps our sex life going strong.

Chris, 42, dentist

You can't lie down in the water. For that reason, I don't like sex in the water. I want to be on top. I want to rule her world. When I am inside her, I want to feel her wetness, not the water.

Brian, 25, utility worker

Water will cause you to rub a blister on your penis quicker than trying to fuck a dry pussy. I find that water takes all the natural lubrication out. In my opinion, sometimes you really can be too clean for sex.

Heath, 39, pharmacist

9. Automobile sex? Driving down the road or parked?

I like to drive down the road fingering my girlfriend. It doesn't really matter where we are going or what time of day it is. I just like to get her all hot and bothered and then stimulate her to orgasm. It gives her something to look forward to, and I really like to lick her juices off my fingers and taste her sex.

Bobby, 23, dry cleaner

My girlfriend loves to give me oral sex when we ride around the countryside in my convertible. She keeps an extra sweater in the backseat to cover her head as she bobs up and down in my lap. And you know what, I've noticed a lot of other convertibles seem to have sweaters in the backseats, too. Just look the next time you're in a parking lot.

Kyle, 26, assistant coach

Although it's been a while since we've done it, my girlfriend loves to climb in the backseat of our Oldsmobile and fuck just like we did in high school. She says it keeps her interested in sex. I think she wants to relive her youthful days. I enjoy it, so I don't complain too much.

Jeffery, 48, auto sales

17 Voyeurism/ Exhibitionism/ Group Sex

1. ***Are you an exhibitionist?***
2. ***Have you ever knowingly had sex with your partner in front of anyone else? If so, did you like it?***
3. ***Have you ever been caught having sex?***
4. ***Are you a voyeur? Your mate?***
5. ***Have you ever watched another couple have sex (not a movie)?***
6. ***Have you ever had multiple partners or an orgy?***
7. ***Have you ever fantasized about a threesome with another woman?***
8. ***Have you ever fantasized about a threesome with another man?***

1. Are you an exhibitionist?

I work out about five days a week. I take good care of my body, and I care about my appearance. I'm not in love with myself, but I do like myself a lot. I like to show off my body at the beach, and I like it when babes check out the bulge in my shorts and the curve of my ass. Does that make me an exhibitionist? If I could go around nude and not get arrested, I probably would.

Walter, 28, traffic cop

My girlfriend likes me to wear supershort cutoff jeans when we go out jogging. She gets a thrill watching other people admire my ass. As long as she's happy, it doesn't really bother me. So I guess I'm a passive exhibitionist, with very tight buns.

Eric, 19, student

No, definitely not, but I'm not a prude either. I am just an ordinary guy who tries to take care of himself. But if I see you looking at my privates, I can make it jump up and down.

Arthur, 36, computer repair

2. Have you ever knowingly had sex with your partner in front of anyone else? If so, did you like it?

Once I got so drunk and high that I let my date talk me into trying an orgy. I have to admit it was very erotic. I know I climaxed five times that night with her. I did not do it with anyone else there, but I gave her a performance she will never forget. We still participate in orgies, but we only have sex with each other. Call us faithful perverts.

Bob, 26, stockman

My girlfriend likes to have sex in front of a life-size stand-up poster of Elvis Presley. Does that count?

Wayne, 44, fishing instructor

3. Have you ever been caught having sex?

My mother caught me with my hands down the pants of my girlfriend once while we were watching TV. I think she was more embarrassed than we were. She told me to take my girlfriend home and to be sure to wash my hands before I came back. I thought it was a pretty weird thing to say at the time, and twenty years later I still do.

Tony, 37, city administrator

In college, my frat had a requirement that you had to be seen having sex or you were on the shit list. They actually kept a master list of pledges. You had to be seen by at least two people, and you had to be having sex with a living, breathing human female. I guess some guys tried to bring their pets or play with plastic love dolls. Since this was pre-AIDS, it wasn't hard to talk girls into helping out. All it took for some guys was the promise to let them come to our regular beer bashes. I had a regular girlfriend, so we just fucked on the pool table in the basement. It seems kinda crude looking back on it, but at the time it seemed perfectly normal to have sex in a room full of drunk college kids.

Alex, 43, internal medicine

Luckily, no. I would probably become a monk if I were ever caught having sex. That is something that should be kept private between two adults.

Cory, 57, janitor

4. Are you a voyeur? Your mate?

My lover has told me about watching other people having sex and how exciting it was. I have never done it, but I'm open-minded, so maybe I'll try it tomorrow night if she's willing and we can find anyone in our neighborhood horny enough to actually have sex.

Charles, 35, diesel-truck repair

The new couple across the courtyard likes to play in their bathroom window. I don't care much about seeing him naked, but she has a great set of jugs. She caught me watching her dry off last week and she waved to me. I'm not sure what I'm supposed to do next. She can't be a day over fifty.

Ernie, 66, retired pilot

My wife likes to listen to our neighbors fuck. It started out as a joke when the banging through the walls became louder than the TV. Now I think she actually looks forward to hearing their sexual noises. Maybe she's just amazed that there are people in our building who aren't too tired to fuck.

Nelson, 34, transportation engineer

5. Have you ever watched another couple have sex (not a movie)?

I had the misfortune and good luck of seeing my grandparents have sex when I was eleven years old. I was spending the summer on their farm, and one night when they thought I had long been asleep, I sneaked out the window of my bedroom to play spy. When I looked through their bedroom window, I saw my sixty-five-year-old grandfather shaking their four-poster bed with his energetic thrusts. I knew I wasn't supposed to be watching, but I couldn't take my eyes away. I can remember seeing his bottom bounce up and down in his white long johns. I can still hear my grandmother telling him to give it to her hot and hard. Ever since then I've had the knowledge that I come from a long line of energetic fuckers.

James, 40, chemical engineer

I grew up in a house with eight kids, my parents, my aunt and uncle, and for several years, my grandparents. People stayed together as families longer back then. I grew up hearing farts, belches, arguments, secrets, and lots of squeaking beds. Somebody was always in the middle of something embarrassing. You learn a lot about life in a home full of relatives.

Jerome, 51, agriculture agent

My lover and I have watched our next-door neighbors screw on their living-room floor. They have watched us in the kitchen. We secretly try to outlast each other in duration. One night I'm sure we're going to invite them over and have an all-nighter. I can't wait.

Fred, 32, teacher

6. Have you ever had multiple partners or an orgy?

Weekly. I always use condoms and practice safe sex. I love the thrill of exploding in several rear ends or hot twats in one night. The more the merrier. I don't even mind other guys screwing the same girl at the same time. I am very open and proud of it. I had my share of monogamous relationships and they all failed, so now I'm just having fun.

Tom, 41, metal engineer

Back in the seventies, my wife and I were swingers. We lost count of sexual partners after we hit the two hundred mark. We made friends all over the country and always had a nice place to vacation whenever we wanted. We got to be very intimate with people we would never have met in the course of our normal activities. Once we got over the initial feelings of insecurity about seeing each other have physical sex with other people, it was quite an adventure. I don't have any regrets. Most of the swingers we met were nice, intelligent, and enjoyed the finer things in life. Despite the fact that we always used condoms and practiced safe sex, once AIDS hit the swingers world ended. I feel sorry for all the younger couples who only know the modern version of orgies. Today's activities must seem like a Hollywood version or an amazing re-creation of something long gone.

George, 63, retired land developer

7. Have you ever fantasized about a threesome with another woman?

I would love to have sex with my girlfriend and her mom. My girlfriend is often mistaken for her mother's sister, and her mom is certainly one sexy woman. She is in her early forties, but she looks like a twenty-year-old cheerleader. I would love to get the two of them together and rock out. I'd have intercourse with one and give head to the other. Then switch positions. It would be great. I know it will never happen, but a guy can dream, can't he?

Ben, 24, factory worker

I have a tough enough time keeping my wife happy, much less worrying about the of yet another woman wanting more than I've got to give.

Ernest, 40, tailor

What red-blooded American boy has not fantasized about a threesome with two women? Yes, I have thought about it for years. I know my girl would not go for it, so I'll keep dreaming about it.

Jeff, 26, disc jockey

8. Have you ever fantasized about a threesome with another man?

This may sound sick, but yes, I have. I want to have another man fuck my girl in the front while I get her rear end. It would make me feel better. I recently discovered she has screwed around on me. I want to fuck her like she just fucked me. Then I'll walk away from the whole damn thing.

Jared, 37, long distance trucker

I have dreamed about having a threesome with my girlfriend and a she-male. I'd like to find a totally feminine chick with a penis and wear her out. We'd try all the mathematical possibilities, and I'd probably wind up sucking my first cock. But if the cock owned a great pair of firm tits and rock-hard nipples, I wouldn't mind so much.

Wesley, 25, communications engineer

If I wanted to suck a guy off and have my girlfriend watch, she'd leave me in a second, and I wouldn't blame her.

Sherman, 30, candymaker

18 Same-Sex Fantasies & Experiences

1. ***Have you ever fantasized about being solo with another man?***
2. ***Have you ever fantasized about a man while having sex with a woman?***
3. ***Has any man ever tried to seduce you? If so, did it flatter you (even if you declined), or did it make you angry?***
4. ***Have you ever made love to another man?***
5. ***Do gay women interest you at all?***
6. ***Would you like to see two women having sex with each other?***
7. ***Would you like to see two men having sex with each other?***

1. Have you ever fantasized about being solo with another man?

I'm not sure. I have this fantasy about doing it with a shemale. I like the outward appearance of a totally beautiful woman, but the idea of sucking a penis really gets me hard. I want big tits, long red hair, smooth skin, wet lips, and an eight-inch cock. I like the idea of it being a secret between the two of us.

Jeff, 25, political analyst

The idea makes me want to run and hide in an orgy of willing, moist women.

Ray, 40, gardener

Never in a million years. I like breasts and hot, wet clits too much to think about being with a man.

Frank, 25, graduate student

From the point of intellectual curiosity I have thought about having sex with another man. But I've also imagined what it would be like to give birth or inhabit the body of a cheetah. I guess I have too much time on my hands.

Rob, 30, librarian

2. Have you ever fantasized about a man while having sex with a woman?

Yes. I wondered what it would be like to have sex with one woman and two other men. I want to see her filled to the brim at all entrances. I only want to try it once, to say that I have done it.

Terrance, 19, stock clerk

I thought about kissing a man once while I was screwing my girlfriend. I was getting ready to climax and I wanted to chill out and make the ride last a little longer. I got an image in my head of kissing my best friend, Sonny, hard on the lips. I don't know where it came from. I don't know why I thought such a thing. I do know it upset me so much, I went limp and didn't come at all.

Randy, 23, horse groomer

I thought about Jesus Christ once when I had an intense orgasm. I saw this beautiful image of his face as clear as day. I must have had a total look of shock on my face because my girlfriend asked me what was wrong. I told her that I just loved her so much it scared me. She gave me a big kiss and we started making love again. I wasn't sure how I felt. I had just lied to my girl while fantasizing about Our Lord at the precise moment I filled her with my sperm. Sounds pretty sick to me. They say God works in mysterious ways. I thought maybe it meant my girl was pregnant, but she started her period a few days later. I guess God was just having a little bit of fun at my expense that day.

Michael, 28, professional bull rider

3. Has any man ever tried to seduce you? If so, did it flatter you (even if you declined), or did it make you angry?

When I was much younger, a coworker had a crush on me. He was about fifteen years older than me, but very handsome, and very macho. I had never had a homosexual relationship and was too set in my prejudices to even consider his advances. We never did anything sexually, though I did flirt and tease him rather shamelessly. I guess I was a weird version of a prick tease, only I actually had a prick to tease with. He died from AIDS in the early nineties, so I'm very thankful that we never did anything. I will admit to being mildly tempted by his repeated offers.

Jason, 42, chef

Back in the seventies, I used to go to adult bookstores and let men suck me off. They'd meet me back at the film booths and follow me into the little closets to watch the movies. I'd lean up against the wall, take out my dick, watch the action on the screen, and let the guy give me a blow job. I'd climax in their mouths, and sometimes they'd give me ten bucks. They usually didn't say a word to me. It was pretty bizarre and mechanical. I never told my girlfriends anything about it. Some of those guys could really give great head! I sometimes wonder what happened to them.

Harvey, 46, express-delivery driver

One time in my life I got real drunk and messed up on cocaine with a longtime friend. We started coming on to this girl in the bar and ended up in a sleazy motel with her. One thing led to another, and before we could do anything, she passed out. We were both so horny that we decided to give each other the release we both needed. He started by touching my penis. After the initial shock, I gave in to the desires that were overpowering my senses. I returned favor for favor, and I'm ashamed to admit it, but it was close to the best sex I've ever had. The climax from being fucked in the ass is so very different from that with a woman. After we left the motel, we didn't mention the night again for weeks. Recently he made some jokes about doing it again. I am not too sure though. I am afraid I'll turn gay even though I still love to fuck women. Maybe I'm bisexual and don't want to admit it.

Jesse, 33, pianist

4. Have you ever made love to another man?

The very idea of another man touching my pecker is revolting. I would have to deck him if he even suggested it.

Ted, 39, realtor

I do it all the time. I love a good stiff dick up my ass. I practice safe sex almost every night of the week. A woman has never been able to please me. I've tried to have sex with them, but I can't seem to have the same type of climax as I do with a man. Their curves and smooth skin turn me off. I like a hairy thigh and a tight butt.

Jesse, 24, artist

5. Do gay women interest you at all?

I love gay women because the ones I know are so dramatic and flamboyant. They have a flair for creativity, and they really enjoy many of the same things that I enjoy. I just hate it when they try to put the move on my girlfriend. There should be some rules of sexual etiquette.

Ron, 30, makeup artist

If they are pretty, sure. If they aren't, who cares? I figure the pretty ones are missing some great dick, and the ugly ones were never going to get any anyway, so no big loss.

Gary, 24, housepainter

The violent man-haters scare me. I know they'd like to get me drunk and then cut my penis off with a dull razor blade. I'm interested in staying away from them, and that's about it.

Chuck, 32, mall security guard

Some of my best friends are gay women, but they don't interest me at all sexually.

Fred, 35, book salesman

6. Would you like to see two women having sex with each other?

Yes, I like to see two women with each other. They seem to know each other's needs. They know how to touch each other to get the quickest and deepest responses. I'm sure they could teach me a lot about lovemaking.

Jordan, 24, short order cook

That is a perversion. *I* want to have the sex with her. A woman should stick with us men. Another woman can only give her a dildo. I've got the real meat hanging between my legs, ready and able to please.

Toby, 21, movie usher

Seeing two sexy women please each other makes me harder than nearly anything. I know in real life they would take one look at my skinny butt and laugh me out of the room. But in my fantasies I enter their bed and they surrender their charms and devote their entire lives to making me happy. If your dreams can't be fantastic, why even bother with them?

Keith, 18, student

7 Would you like to see two men having sex with each other?

The idea of men sucking each other makes me want to puke and get violent. Maybe I'm not sensitive enough to my masculine desires, but I don't care. I have zero tolerance for homosexual sex, and the entire idea makes my skin crawl.

Steve, 27, construction worker

I like the force and passion of gay sex. They get down to business and don't stop until they are done. I like the directness of their approach. They don't have to be sensitive and waste all that time with foreplay. They just pump until they explode.

Dustin, 38, accountant

I have never thought about it, but it might be a turn-on. I've heard how forceful they are and how they can be quite primitive with each other. Just pure animalistic sex. I am not gay or anything, but I would like to see it just once.

Arnold, 34, rights activist

19 Fetishes

1. ***Do you have any fetishes?***
2. ***Does your partner have any fetishes?***
3. ***Does forceful sex appeal to you?***
4. ***Do you like bondage?***
5. ***Do you like sex mixed with pain?***
6. ***Do you ever give or receive any bruises from sexual experiences?***
7. ***Do you have a fetish for women's feet?***
8. ***Do you like to spank or be spanked?***
9. ***Do you like to be bitten?***
10. ***Do you like hickeys?***
11. ***What's the kinkiest sex you have ever had?***
12. ***Are you kinky?***

1. Do you have any fetishes?

I have always loved the feel of silk panties against my skin. I used to steal my older sister's all the time, and even when she caught me red-handed, with them literally around my waist, I would deny, deny, deny. I know it is more than the simple feel of silk that turns me on, because silk boxers or male silk briefs just leave me cold. They have to be pretty, frilly panties manufactured for women or I'm just not interested.

Carl, 41, business manager

My girl knows how much I love to wear her high heels around the house. She only gets mad when I wear them too much and stretch the leather.

Vic, 32, limo driver

The only fetish I have is that I love to see my lover in a short, sexy negligee before bedtime. I love to see what's underneath. Long gowns and robes do nothing for me.

Tim, 26, horse jockey

I like leather and chrome, on my cars, my furniture, and my women.

Alex, 40, importer

2. Does your partner have any fetishes?

If she does, she hasn't let me in on it. Maybe she's too scared of disapproval to tell me. Maybe she feels like I will think she is weird and not love her.

Gerome, 23, telemarketer

My wife likes to go around the house in my shirts and boxers. I think that's strange. She says they're comfortable. Maybe she thinks comfortable, I'll go with plain ole sexy. I won't leave her alone when she wears them.

Brett, 37, furniture refinisher

My girlfriend likes to pinch me. I don't mean little, light taps. I mean hard grabs of skin that leave marks on my arms, legs, and ass. I think she plays too rough. She usually calls me a sissy and pinches me even harder. I'm not sure if she's mean. I'm not sure if I'm being abused. I'm not sure if I even like it or that I should want to like it.

Sean, 31, graphic designer

3. Does forceful sex appeal to you?

I like to be forceful sometimes when my girlfriend is in the mood. If she is properly lubricated and has had sufficient foreplay, I can ravish her with total lust. I pound a hole in her and have actually fucked the shit out of her before. She says that she likes to be overwhelmed by me.

Brandon, 24, manager trainee

Force and sex do not go together. I never understood how a rapist could get an erection, knowing the woman didn't want him. I have to know that the woman I'm with wants me and welcomes my attention, or I just lose my hard-on. I could never force myself on a woman.

Jeff, 29, illustrator

The only way forceful sex appeals to me is if my lover is willing to participate. If he wants it hard, then he gets it hard. He lets me know exactly how he wants me to love him. If I were to be too rough with him and he didn't want it that way, he would leave me. I'd just die if he left me.

Jamie, 21, night clerk

4. Do you like bondage?

The idea of tying up a girl and ravishing her body is very appealing. I would never hurt her. I would be very gentle unless she liked it forceful. Then I could vibrate the walls. I'd rock her world and make her beg me to take her harder. Some fantasy. I can't wait to fulfill it.

Allen, 35, orthopedic assistant

I enjoy being tied up by my girlfriend. I like the thrill of not knowing what she is going to do to me. She teases me unmercifully. She makes me beg for her. I love the animal in her. I like the way she makes me whimper.

Keith, 30, diamond broker

I am so bound and gagged by my bills, mortgage, obligations, and responsibilities, the idea of getting physically tied up in leather simply doesn't appeal to me at all. Whatever the total opposite of bondage is, that's what I'm looking for.

Bart, 41, claims adjuster

5. Do you like sex mixed with pain?

My wife likes to squeeze my balls right when I'm getting ready to come. It seems to have a turbocharge effect on me if she does it with the right force. If she does it wrong, it hurts like hell. Sometimes it makes me want to pass out from the pain.

Wayne, 43, truck driver

I like to fuck until I feel like someone put my balls in a vise and twisted them. I know I've had a good night of sex.

Tracy, 30, car salesman

That is the only way to have sex with me. The more painful, the better I like it. Please whip me and tell me what a dog I am. I want her to treat me like shit. She makes me lick her shoes. If I am good, I get my reward. Fabulous, degrading sex. Bring on the leather whip.

Kirk, 24, glass installer

6. Do you ever give or receive any bruises from sexual experiences?

My girlfriend bruises easily, I have to treat her like a china doll. Sometime we get a little carried away during sex, and the next day she will look like she's been in World War III. I always feel bad, but she doesn't complain.

Colby, 32, auto detailer

My wife beats me up mentally and emotionally every day. I always have a killer headache. Life with her is a big pain. Sex just plain hurts. I don't know why I put myself through all the grief. I tell myself I endure it because of the children, but they are miserable, too. Someone needs to end the cycle, but I doubt if I'll be the one to do it.

Jordan, 29, retailer

My girlfriend and I kiss each other so much our lips are constantly chapped and swollen. We wear our puffy sores like proud badges of honor.

Bradley, 19, student

7. Do you have a fetish for women's feet?

Other than propping them up on my shoulders when I'm having sex, I couldn't care less about my girlfriend's feet.

As long as they get her where she wants to go, they are fine with me.

Robert, 20, office worker

I like to let my girlfriend rub my pecker with her feet. She puts my tool between her silk-covered toes and captures my total attention. She calls it exercise. I call it a good time.

Frank, 24, law student

I like to look at girls' feet if they're sexy, but I don't kiss them or anything like that.

Juan, 29, medical intern

8. Do you like to spank or be spanked?

My wife likes it when I spank her on the bottom a few times with my leather belt. It gets her wet in record time. I, on the other hand, will not tolerate being hit during sex even by accident.

Cecil, 45, auto dealer

I like to put the fear of God in my wife by threatening to spank her when she has been too free with the credit cards or bought one too many party dresses. One night I might just pull her fancy silk panties down to her knees and wear her fanny out with my hand. It might be fun, as long as she doesn't press charges or get her asshole brother, the lawyer, involved.

Derek, 36, property manager

I love it when my wife disciplines me. She is quite good at playing the part. She keeps a cane switch in the closet and makes me soak it in hot water before she delivers my richly deserved punishment every month or so. She keeps a list of my naughty deeds, and when I've committed ten infractions, down come my trousers. I admit that sometimes I purposely make a few boo-boos to reach the magic number. I love the way she holds my erect penis in her black satin gloves after she has brought tears to my eyes with her cane.

Nicholas, 41, trust fund administrator

9. Do you like to be bitten?

I like soft bites on my butt. Maybe it is some repressed memory from my baby crib, but I love it when my wife gets playful and nips my butt. I'm not talking about taking out a big chunk. I just mean a little teasing.

Juan, 28, restaurant manager

My former girlfriend was playing around one day and she bite my balls harder than I would have liked her to. I thought I was going to pass out. All action came to a complete stop, and I just wanted to cry. I didn't want sex for another month. It took even longer for me to completely start trusting her again.

Simon, 42, policeman

I like when my wife lightly bites me on the head of my penis. Just a little nip at times. At times I will lovingly bite her clit. It gets us both very hot.

Jerry, 40, roofer

10. Do you like hickeys?

I think they are disgusting teenage-petting leftovers from the eighties. I don't like them and will not put one on my girl.

Hugh, 52, transmission specialist

I like to suck my wife's neck until it looks like a leech attacked her. I call it "putting my mark on her." At least it isn't permanent like the tattoo I want her to put on her right tit.

Brandon, 25, stage actor

11. What's the kinkiest sex you have ever had?

When I fucked two girls anally in the back of my cab. I picked them up at the same time. They were real hot and wanted me to do both of them. I aim to please and was glad to do my civic duty. It was great, but both had very tight butts. I really enjoyed it, but my pecker hurt for several days.

Gil, 36, taxi driver

12. Are you kinky?

If it feels good, I do it. If it feels weird, I'll try it.

Saul, 34, events planner

The longer I'm in a relationship, the kinkier I get. Maybe I just get bored, but after about a year or so, I get the urge to experiment with fruit, windup toys, chains, and things that strap on. Then the relationship usually falls apart, and I start all over again.

Barry, 45, business consultant

It depends on what is considered kinky. I've had sex in the swimming pool with my girl and two friends. The other girl would not participate fully, so me and the other guy took my girl at the same time. I fucked her in the ass while he screwed her in front. It was thrilling. Now we do this at least every other week. My girl is open to anything. Does that make me kinky?

Ray, 28, radio announcer

20 Experimentation

1. ***What do you do to keep your sex life interesting and enjoyable?***
2. ***What is the wildest thing you've ever talked your partner into doing sexually?***
3. ***What is the wildest thing your partner has ever talked you into doing sexually?***
4. ***Do you like anal sex?***
5. ***What does your partner think about anal sex?***
6. ***Have you ever done anything sexually one time that you would never do again?***
7. ***What was the experience your mate initiated that you hated, but once you were on your way, you loved?***
8. ***Who initiates new sexual adventures in lovemaking, you or your mate?***

1. What do you do to keep your sex life interesting and enjoyable?

Maybe it is simply my fear of commitment, but I tend to end my relationships when the sex gets stale. Or maybe the sex gets stale because I know the relationship is over. Whatever, it always ends the same way. I don't get bored with sex because I am always changing partners.

Wayne, 35, investment planner

I concentrate on keeping my wife happy. Sure, after all these years we have done almost every position in every room of our house, but it still feels great. I still breathe air every day, and I still make love to my wife the same basic way I did fifteen years ago. The best sex I ever had is the sex I just had.

Marvin, 63, aviation mechanic

I do whatever it takes to keep my wife happy in bed and out of bed. If she is happy out of bed, then she is happier in bed. It can be as simple as taking extra time with foreplay. Simple maybe, but it works for us.

Richie, 45, gynecologist

2. What is the wildest thing you've ever talked your partner into doing sexually?

I once talked my lover into doing coke with me and screwing several men at one time. She was higher than a kite and really got into it. There were four of us guys and she satisfied every one of us. I think it was her secret fantasy to be a slut for a night. She fucked me and one guy at the same time, while jerking off one with her hand and one in her mouth. I love her and I am still with her. Besides, it was my fault, because I asked her to do it.

Benjamin, 32, band director

I talked my boyfriend into going with me to a straight bar, where we picked up two hetero women and took them back to our apartment. We did our best imitations of macho men and actually convinced the girls to go into our bedroom for a night of sex. Once we all got naked on our big double bed, John and I got into a tight 69 position and just sucked each other until we came in each other's mouth. The girls sat there watching at first. My date turned red, got mad, and called me a "fucking faggot," which at that particular moment I certainly was. She slammed a wine bottle into the wall and broke one of my picture frames. She jerked on her clothes and told Rachel to come on with her. Rachel proved to be quite a willing little fag hag. She not only ignored her friend's pleas to leave, she took my dick in her mouth and started her version of oral sex. I almost forgave the fact that she had a vagina. That little girl sucked me off like a gay lumberjack. Her daddy would have been so proud.

Trent, 24, freelance fashion consultant

3. What is the wildest thing your partner has ever talked you into doing sexually?

My girlfriend convinced me that buying her a mink coat would make our sex life better. I guess as long as she believes it will, it will. It's kind of a self-fulfilling prophecy. I'm sure her next turn-on will be a new convertible.

Bruno, 50, labor specialist

Letting her do it with another man and woman. I could watch but I was not allowed to touch her or anyone else. It was a weird turn-on. I got an immediate erection. She flaunted herself shamelessly within inches of my face. She finally gave herself to me and I screwed her until she begged for mercy. It was thrilling to show the bitch who was better in bed.

Bradford, 25, hotel waiter

4. Do you like anal sex?

I don't know, because I have never tried it. I'm not gay. I may try it at some point in my life, but the girl I'm with now will not let me do her in the rear.

Max, 28, laborer

We were going at it hot and heavy when my wife suggested a vibrator. I was turned on so I said okay. Little did I know that she wanted to shove it up my butt. She started putting it in me slow and easy. At first I was scared, but I had to admit it was feeling good. After a few minutes she was literally butt-fucking me with the thing while I was fucking her. We both exploded at the same time. We now own two and they are always close to the bed.

Josh, 24, waiter

5. What does your partner think about anal sex?

My girlfriend doesn't even trust me enough to bend over around me anymore. Two months ago, I made the mistake of trying to have anal sex with her before she was properly lubricated, and she still hasn't forgiven me. I was drunk and horny, she wasn't. I even offered to let her stick a dildo up my butt for paybacks, but she just told me to go away.

Matthew, 23, lifeguard

My wife likes to have anal sex about once a month as a special treat. She uses it as a reward and as an enticement to get me to be a good boy. It works. She can be shopping at the mall, see something on sale, wiggle her little butt in my direction, and I fold like a house of cards. I'm a slave to her ass.

Andrew, 34, travel agent

My partner enjoys anal sex. She is well lubricated and turned on before we ever start, and I have to be semihard to enter her. Once we get started, she wants it hard, fast, and the deeper the better. I worry about breaking my dick when we go at it so hard sometimes.

Dan, 30, auto parts sales

6. Have you ever done anything sexually one time that you would never do again?

In a drunken stupor I let my girlfriend pee in my mouth. I don't remember it tasting that bad. I don't remember much about it at all, but she always uses it as an example of how stupid I get when I party too much. It's pretty hard to argue with her when she's right.

Theo, 20, student

My girlfriend talked me into a threesome with a total stranger and it ruined our relationship. I thought I was a big, strong, secure guy, but seeing her with another man broke my heart. And even though I know it was just physical, meaningless sex, I can't get over it. She wants to try a threesome with another woman, but I'm not sure if I even want to go out with her again, much less share her with yet another person.

Howard, 25, motel clerk

Yes, once I let my love talk me into a play rape. I got so turned on that I got carried away. But when I saw the fear in her eyes, I quickly lost my erection. With that bad experience, I have never tried it again.

Ricky, 21, law student

7. What was the experience your mate initiated that you hated, but once you were on your way, you loved?

I didn't originally like the idea of being spanked. It seemed humiliating and dumb. I didn't like it when I was a kid, and I didn't think I would like it as a grown man. I was wrong. The first time my wife played dress-up in her black leather shoes and fishnet hose and told me to bend over her lap, I got an erection that wouldn't go down. Three sharp whacks from her hot-pink-fingernailed hand was all it took to make me ejaculate.

Kenneth, 39, surveyor

The first time I gave a girl oral sex scared me to death. I was eighteen and I knew I was supposed to like the idea, but when the actual moment met me right up in my face, I thought I would pass out. I started out licking everywhere but where she needed my attention. I took the most scenic route to a woman's vagina any man has ever taken. She was beyond ready, and I was still nibbling on her belly button. She finally took my head and rammed me into her groin. I gasped for air, thought I was going to drown, and then took my first big lick. The taste was overwhelming, but wonderful. I loved the taste. Really, really loved it. I made up for lost time. I gulped and almost tried to climb up inside her. Her juice ran all down my neck. My hair was totally soaked. It was religious. It was just the thought of sucking her pee hole that caused me so much concern. Who knew how wonderful it would turn out to be?

Carl, 25, pool man

Going to bed with two guys. My lover talked me into it while we were well into the act of having sex. He ask if a friend could join us and I said sure, and so this friend of his joined us in bed. I enjoyed being the object of two men's desires. I would do it all over again if given the chance. It was very stimulating and athletic.

Tyrone, 21, unemployed

8. Who initiates new sexual adventures in lovemaking, you or your mate?

Without a doubt my mate takes charge. I am happy with the old missionary position, but she thinks variety is the spice of life. I usually go along because I just want to get laid.

Mark, 39, machine operator

It always seems like she wants to try something new right when we are already in the middle of sex. We have to stop and start all over. I wish she would be more natural and go with the flow.

Ryan, 56, airport baggage handler

If one of her girlfriends reads about it in a book or hears something new on a talk show, somehow my wife volunteers to let us be the first in her group to test it out. I never know what to expect when I walk in the bedroom. I can always tell by her weird little smile that the night is going to be unusual. You gotta love her spirit of adventure.

Owen, 42, road inspector

21 Sex, Drugs & Alcohol

1. ***Does alcohol make sex better or worse?***
2. ***Do you have trouble getting erect when you have been drinking?***
3. ***What is the best experience you have had with alcohol and sex?***
4. ***What is the worst experience you have had with alcohol and sex?***
5. ***Do you use drugs for sexual enhancement?***
6. ***What is the best experience you have had with drugs and sex?***
7. ***What is the worst experience you have had with drugs and sex?***

1. Does alcohol make sex better or worse?

I believe that alcohol makes me feel better, and when I feel better, I act more confidently. I've always had a few beers on dates. I like to have a pitcher or two when I'm out barhopping, so maybe I just use alcohol as a crutch. One night I was out with the guys and they switched our beer over to non-alcoholic versions without telling me. I didn't notice anything different, and my come-on lines were just as stupid. So maybe I don't need alcohol after all.

Ray, 20, assembly-line worker

In my experience, most women like a little wine before sex to warm them up. Not enough to make them sick, but enough to make them relax and shed their inhibitions.

Mark, 34, advertising executive

Personally, if I am only having a few drinks, I am more amorous.

Howard, 26, factory worker

2. Do you have trouble getting erect when you have been drinking?

Only when I am so drunk the room is spinning, otherwise it has no effect on my erections.

Jeffrey, 36, life insurance sales

Alcohol makes me hornier than hell. I can fuck anything in sight if I want to. I've never had a problem with booze and erections. Knock on my woody.

Noah, 29, dentist

When I'm drunk, my pecker thinks every woman in the place is a fucking goddess. That sometimes leads to reality problems when I sober up and see who is curled up in some bed beside me.

Lyle, 23, tobacco farmer

3. What is the best experience you have had with alcohol and sex?

The best experience I've had with alcohol and sex was when my girlfriend got drunk enough to give me oral sex for the first time. She had denied me for over a year, and then one night of drunken bliss she decided to do the deed. What is even better is that she continues to do it now that she is sober. She said the first time was the hardest. Now she goes down on me like a vacuum cleaner.

Butch, 23, travel planner

My best time with sex and alcohol occurred a few years ago in college when I got too drunk to have an erection. I passed out on the floor while my so-called best friend had sex with my so-called date. She had herpes and gave it to him. I heard him whine about it for two full years until we finally graduated and went our separate ways.

Robert, 25, stock researcher

If my memory serves me, it was when I was shipping in the navy and I met this chick in a bar. We went to a motel and fucked the night away while drinking tequila. It was pure sex and nothing else. I never saw her again.

Chad, 34, navy SEAL

4. What is the worst experience you have had with alcohol and sex?

Once when I was trying to impress this date, I got so blindly drunk I threw up on her as I was performing oral sex. She got pissed off. I passed out. I barely made it back to the barracks. I have not seen her since.

Gary, 24, military policeman

When I get drunk, I can't remember names. Dates don't like this habit of mine. They seem to take it personally for some odd reason. I usually say fuck 'em, but then I call them by someone else's name, which I find quite humorous. They never laugh as much as I do about it.

Joe, 30, telephone repairman

5. Do you use drugs for sexual enhancement?

No. I have such an obsessive personality I'm afraid that if I used something like cocaine, I'd lose all interest in everything else. I have enough problems as it is.

Phil, 20, premed student

I owe my marriage, home, and three nearly grown children to a nickel bag of marijuana. I got my future wife high on our first date twenty-five years ago, and we had such a good time fucking and loving that we never stopped. If she hadn't been such a sex kitten on our first date, we might not even have had a second date. She told me later that I was her first sexual partner and that night was her first time to smoke pot. If things hadn't turned out so great for us, I might feel a little guilty about taking advantage of her.

Fred, 44, career counselor

I have never tried drugs for sexual pleasure. I'm not sure I would even know what to use. Any ideas?

Jake, 21, medical student

6. What is the best experience you have had with drugs and sex?

To me sex is a drug. When I have sex, I am on a natural high. When I don't have sex, I get depressed.

Kirk, 31, physical education teacher

I used cocaine on a girlfriend's clit one time. We were able to go for a very long time. We drank of each other. We had sex in every position that night. We fucked and fucked till she was drier than a busted oil well. After that we were too sore to touch each other for a week. I never did cum that night, though I did have a blast trying to finish.

Matt, 29, bank teller

7. What is the worst experience you have had with drugs and sex?

I got high with a bunch of semifamous musicians one night and made a complete ass of myself. I took three hits off their skunk water bong and started talking like a college professor about stuff that I knew absolutely nothing about. The girl who had previously seemed very interested in touching my shoulder and holding my knee disappeared with the sound guy. By the time I finished munching out on the band's backstage vegetable platter, I was all alone and stranded without a ride home. That is the night drugs killed my sex life.

Eric, 19, T-shirt vendor

When I do drugs, I don't care about sex.

Robert, 27, commercial painter

I recall one time period in my life when I used drugs quite heavily, I screwed anything in a skirt. I am lucky that I never caught a disease. I get my blood tested every three months now and I no longer use drugs.

Perry, 27, mechanic

22 Inhibitions

1. ***If no one was looking, what would you be apt to do sexually that you have never done before?***
2. ***What sexual subject would you love to talk about but can't?***
3. ***What do men have a hard time asking for from a woman?***
4. ***Are you always honest with your lover about what you want sexually?***
5. ***What do women have a hard time asking for from a man?***
6. ***Do you think your lover is always honest with you about what she wants sexually?***
7. ***Have you ever had a sexual experience that was too embarrassing to enjoy?***
8. ***If a sexual experience is embarrassing, but feels great, do you keep it on your sexual menu?***

1. If no one was looking, what would you be apt to do sexually that you have never done before?

If nobody would ever find out, I'd have sex with Sherry at work. Her long blond hair and hot red lips drive me crazy. I know it isn't really a big deal for blacks and whites to date these days, but my family would disown me. My parents raised me to be proud of my black heritage. We were always required to know our roots, as well as Alex Haley's. I have always dated women of color, but I would just love to know what it feels like to ram my cock deep inside my blue-eyed dream girl just once.

Eugene, 27, research assistant

If I could get away with it, I'd spurt my cum in my supervisor's coffee cup and make her swallow every drop. She is so high and mighty on the job. She makes my life hell. I'd like to have her openly and willingly submit to my sexual demands right on her fancy desk. I know that she'd love me if she'd give me a chance.

Rod, 23, telemarketer

I'd have oral sex with a she-male, if I knew it was safe. I love the idea of tits and a dick on the same person. I'm not gay, I'm just curious.

Larry, 25, tennis instructor

I would try a threesome with two girls. I don't have the guts to ask for it though.

Troy, 21, student

2. What sexual subject would you love to talk about but can't?

I have no problem talking about sex or anything else, period.

Jordan, 36, air-conditioning repairman

I talk about sex for hours. My wife says that I'm addicted to sex. I want it all the time. I do have a problem talking about anal sex. I want to try it, but I'm afraid she will think I'm kinky.

Jed, 27, auto industry

My desire to have my wife swallow my cum is a real hard thing for me to bring up at the dinner table.

Sammy, 34, shoe manufacturer

3. What do men have a hard time asking for from a woman?

I think men want women to be sluttier and free-spirited with them. The old saying that everyone wants a whore in bed is certainly true with me. I want my dates to be nasty, horny, enthusiastic, and lusty. I don't want them to worry about what I might think about them in the morning. I want them to concentrate on the moment and the pleasure. I wish I could tell them what I really want.

Lou, 25, electronics salesman

Men can't take the truth from women, so they put up with amazing amounts of grief and misery. They'd rather fool themselves for years than face the facts about themselves.

Peter, 30, art teacher

I believe men have a hard time asking a woman out for a first date. Men cannot take rejection easily.

George, 23, dump-truck driver

4. Are you always honest with your lover about what you want sexually?

Hell, no, I'm afraid she would laugh at some of my desires.

Royce, 34, graphics designer

I tried to be honest with my partner. She laughed and made fun of me, so I dropped her like a hot potato. I get enough shit at work. I don't need it in my personal life.

Trent, 39, accounting director

I'm never honest. She wouldn't do what I want, so why bother? That is what whores are for.

Clyde, 44, transmission repairman

5. What do women have a hard time asking for from a man?

Nothing. They ask for anything, anytime. And if they don't get it, they stop asking and start demanding.

Herb, 38, schoolteacher

Women will not ask a man to lick their butt holes. I know. I always have to do the asking, and they always tell me how much they enjoyed it when I'm finished. I go where few men dare, and it always pays off for me in bed.

Amos, 45, bartender

I have never met a woman that was scared to ask for anything she really wanted.

Jacob, 25, delivery driver

6. Do you think your lover is always honest with you about what she wants sexually?

I have no idea. I have never had a serious enough relationship with a woman to care if she was being honest about her sexual needs.

Billy, 23, data entry clerk

If a girl is not honest about what she wants in bed, then she's not honest with herself. I want my partner to let me know what and how she wants it. Ask and ye shall receive.

Bart, 41, photographer

Who knows? Who cares? Next question?

Leroy, 19, unemployed

7. Have you ever had a sexual experience that was too embarrassing to enjoy?

I was having sex with this girl once and she kept calling me by the wrong name. She didn't even realize it. I'll admit that we didn't really know each other that well, but we were in the sack making intimate connections, so I would have liked it if she had at least known my name. The sex felt great, but my ears burned every time she called me Tom.

Tim, 22, singing waiter

I loved it when my wife put ice cubes up my anus, then gave me a slow, intense blow job. The combination of extremes made me harder than I'd been in years. I think I liked it too much. Now I'm afraid she'll think I'm a freak if I admit I want her to do it again.

Dirk, 43, truck driver

One time my girlfriend got so excited during sex that she peed on me. She was embarrassed to death, but I actually enjoyed the experience.

Burt, 30, building inspector

One time I let my wife talk me into going to a live sex show in New Orleans. The place was a little dive and the show was horrible. She was turned on and I was just too embarrassed about the whole damn thing to enjoy it.

Jared, 45, dentist

8. If a sexual experience is embarrassing, but feels great, do you keep it on your sexual menu?

Absolutely. If I discovered something new and enjoyed it, I would want to do it again and again.

Joel, 32, store owner

If I came across a new pleasure, I would use it in the future. Life is too short not to experience new things. My mother told me to always be willing to try new things. She said you may find something you'll love.

Joey, 23, reporter

Sometimes the rush of embarrassment is why it feels so good.

Kelsey, 45, investor

23 Love vs. Sex

1. ***What is the biggest difference between making passionate love and having great sex?***
2. ***Do you think it is necessary to be in love with somebody before you sleep with them?***
3. ***Which part of sex is most important to you: cuddling, foreplay, talking afterward, how you are treated after sex, or the physical ins and outs?***
4. ***If you love your mate, but she is not good sexually, what do you do?***
5. ***Do you stick with someone you love and care about, even if the sex is terrible?***
6. ***Is great sex or a good relationship more important? Can you have a great relationship if the sex is bad?***
7. ***Do you understand a woman's emotions and needs?***
8. ***Have you ever been insensitive to a woman's sexual needs and just went after your own desires?***

1. What is the biggest difference between making passionate love and having great sex?

None, if you love the one you're with, how can you say the two are different? I have never been able to have meaningless sex with anyone.

Derrick, 67, retired

Passionate love requires two ingredients: passion and love. Even Bubba can understand this. Now, understanding how to discern the difference between sexual cravings and lust is a monkey of another color.

Stephen, 42, quality control manager

I can have great sex with a total stranger and never know her name. Passionate love usually means that I have to buy flowers and eventually meet her parents.

Theo, 28, media buyer

2. Do you think it is necessary to be in love with somebody before you sleep with them?

If that were the case, a lot of men would never have sex. They don't know what love is, only lust.

Abel, 45, machinist

No. There is lust and there is love. Don't confuse the two. If you are lucky enough to be in lust and love with the same person, great. If not, lust the one you're with and pretend it's love.

Jacob, 28, secretary

I want to be sure they do not have AIDS. I want to see a current health card and hold it in my hands. Other than that, if she is female, has a brain, and speaks English, I'm interested.

I like them pretty, but I really look more for intelligence and chemistry.

Harold, 38, professor

3. Which part of sex is most important to you: cuddling, foreplay, talking afterward, how you are treated after sex, or the physical ins and outs?

I like the physical in and out. My girlfriend would rather I do a lot more cuddling and foreplay. Sometimes I'm in the mood to take my time. But usually it's just the ins and outs, thank you, ma'am.

Hank, 34, computer programmer

Now, what man is going to say the most important part of sex is the cuddling or foreplay? We are men, we have to keep up our image. The thrusting is more important.

Scott, 43, oil rigger

Fucking, fucking, and lots more fucking. That's what men do best. If no one is looking and I completely tell the truth, I love cuddling, foreplay, and how I am treated after sex. It always seems to backfire on me, though. When I show my true colors, the lady I'm with gets possessive and sappy.

Brett, 27, sales

4. If you love your mate, but she is not good sexually, what do you do?

I would try to teach her to be better in bed. If she couldn't to learn, then I guess I would eventually stray and that would end the relationship. Harsh words but true.

Joe, 32, banker

I'd send her to a sex therapist. I'd help her practice. If I had to, I'd buy her a how-to video. But I wouldn't leave her. I would stay with her. I can always use my hand.

Samuel, 48, banker

Dump her. Life is short and my dick is long.

Terry, 32, law enforcement

5. Do you stick with someone you love and care about, even if the sex is terrible?

I have to be truthful. I would find some good ass somewhere else and try to keep her from finding out. Maybe I'm a jerk, but a man has got to have some good sex occasionally.

Kelvin, 46, store owner

It's got to be pretty damn bad before I'll leave, as long as it's plentiful. Keep it wet and ready and I'll make do.

Johnny, 46, home improvement business

6. Is great sex or a good relationship more important? Can you have a great relationship if the sex is bad?

I have had great sex and a great relationship but always with different people. I am still looking for the one that can give me both.

John, 27, sportscaster

I am in that situation right now. I'm still contemplating what to do about my life. I have a good relationship but no sex.

Sloan, 24, unemployed

Both are imperative. Great sex is born out of great love. Great love breeds great sex. I have both in my marriage, but it wasn't easy finding the right woman. I took a few wrong turns on the highway of love.

Adriann, 30, painting contractor

7. Do you understand a woman's emotions and needs?

Since the beginning of time man has tried to understand women. We still don't know them. They are too emotional to understand. So I simply try to get along with them.

Jonathan, 35, insurance sales

Women are human beings. I am of the opinion that understanding women is paramount to understanding yourself, and vice versa.

Pat, 48, physician

Women are like a toy I used to play with as a kid. My little rock-hard Super Ball would bounce off the walls with the slightest effort on my part. Most women are the same way. Just look at them the wrong way, put a little spin on the situation, and they will bounce for hours with absolutely no extra work on my part.

Ethan, 38, clinic worker

8. Have you ever been insensitive to a woman's sexual needs and just went after your own desires?

There is a no man alive who has not at one time or another, been insensitive to a woman's sexual needs. I try not to be, but it's hard at times.

Gerald, 24, waiter

When I have been without sex for a while, I can overlook a woman's needs and desires. A stiff prick often gets in the way of my being a gentleman.

Randy, 33, radio announcer

I don't think about a woman's needs when I'm getting a piece of ass. I am a jerk and proud of it. I usually just want to get laid, not fall in love.

Jeremy, 28, loan officer

Sure. The majority of women I have slept with don't seem to know what they want sexually. The word *clueless* comes to mind. I don't sleep with stupid women, either. That's not what I mean. I just somehow know more about what they want and will enjoy than they do. I'm not complaining, it makes me feel great.

Lonny, 41, restaurant manager

24 Dressing Up

1. ***Do you like to dress in stylish clothes? Describe some of them.***
2. ***What type of underwear does your partner prefer you wear?***
3. ***Does your lover ever cross-dress (dress like a man)?***
4. ***Do you ever cross-dress?***
5. ***What do you like to wear that belongs to your partner?***
6. ***What does your partner like to wear that belongs to you?***

1. Do you like to dress in stylish clothes? Describe some of them.

I have to wear business suits to work all week, so I dress down at home. If I'm going out somewhere special, I'll wear a nice, casual shirt and pants.

Barry, 34, executive

When you are single, you always have to look your best. You never know where you'll meet a chick. My favorite color is basic black. You can dress it up or down. I refuse to wear ties.

Greg, 30, stock market sales

I like to look my best. What a woman wears, how she is packaged, if you will, makes me look and continue to look. I try to do the same for her. Khakis are my favorite. Easy to care for and they look sharp, depending on the shirt worn with them. I can dress them up or down just by changing shirts or adding a tie. I love both clothing and women that are low maintenance.

Bill, 43, banker

I wear one pair of jeans until they fall apart, then I get another pair just like the first ones. I only own a single pair of sneakers at a time, and I have about six shirts I rotate. Since I don't wear any underwear, that pretty much sums up my entire wardrobe. I make my own style, and I travel light.

Jody, 24, stage crew member

2. What type of underwear does your partner prefer you wear?

None comes to mind. My girl likes me to wear nothing at all under my pants. She says she likes the way I fill my pants naturally.

Timothy, 38, HMO vice president

She likes boxers, and particularly soft cotton or flannel. She has always had a taste for soft materials and hard bodies, I suppose. She hates regular men's underwear. Needless to say, I don't wear them anymore.

William, 41, employment counselor

I know I sound like a pervert, but I like G-strings and thongs. I like the way they cradle my jewels and center themselves in my crack. My wife likes to run her hands down my pants when we hug. She likes to grab my cheeks in both hands and thrust me into her embrace.

Anthony, 26, boat seller

If Belinda had her way, I wouldn't wear any—ever. I get ill when my balls ache from scratching up against the material of my pants. I hide my underwear from her so she won't give them to the garbageman.

George, 30, insurance adjuster

3. Does your lover ever cross-dress (dress like a man)?

My wife likes to wear my shirts around the house. I think she is sexy in them, so if you call that cross-dressing, then I guess she does.

William, 35, painter

Only on Halloween.

Craig, 26, salesman

I don't know what I would do if she did. I just can't imagine that. It's too weird to picture. I'd feel in competition, I suppose. I want my woman to look and act entirely like a woman.

John, 51, electrician

She doesn't wear men's clothes. She wears fake men's parts! My baby likes to strap on a rubber dick and make me whimper. My knees get weak when she pulls that black monster out of the cedar chest.

Nigel, 35, neon craftsman

4. Do you ever cross-dress?

I have never put on anything feminine in my life. I am not planning to do so in the future.

Henry, 38, business analyst

Give me a pair of my wife's pantyhose and I'm a happy man. I like the way they're soft and silky against my skin. They make my legs look good, too.

Victor, 32, court clerk

Good God, no. I am very heterosexual. But I have thought about it. That ladies' lingerie store, Somebody's Secret, or whatever it's called, is a really interesting place.

Mark, 27, phone repair technician

I can't fill her bra, and I rip holes out of her panties. What's the point?

Jack, 46, gardener

If I ever even *thought* about cross-dressing, my wife would throw me across the room. And she's bigger by far than I am. No, I do not cross-dress. Besides, isn't that considered a sickness?

Paul, 49, gardener

5. What do you like to wear that belongs to your partner?

The only thing I could ever imagine wearing that belonged to her is maybe her old cotton robe in an emergency.

Bill, 35, medical technician

My girlfriend travels a lot. When she is out of town, I'll put on some of her clothes and step out for the evening. It's fun to see how many men try to pick me up. There's a bunch of sick people out there. I have never left with anyone. I just do it for kicks.

Waylon, 29, truck driver

Her body.

Jeremy, 21, music student

I like to wear one of her scarves around my neck in winter. It keeps me warm and fills my senses with her lovely aroma.

Baxter, 50, international trader

There's something really sexy about wearing women's panties, especially when she knows they're right under my suit. I look all macho on the outside and still have my feminine side lurking underneath.

Charles, 40, dry cleaning business owner

6. What does your partner like to wear that belongs to you?

She wears my tees all the time. They are so long that they actually look like a dress on her. I love the look of her legs coming out from under my T-shirt.

Joel, 27, X-ray technician

She's got this crazy way of taking my underwear and wearing them around the house rolled up on her head. I laugh and then I get excited. I still can't figure out what exactly excites me about that, but it does. She kinda looks like a skinny Aunt Jemima. To each their own, I guess.

Aaron, 32, computer sales

My baby likes to put on my tie before we make love, then lets me put it anywhere I can while we play. I probably have the most crusty ties known to man, and I love them. Each stain brings back such great memories.

Howard, 36, advertising executive

Anything she can get her hands on, whether I'm already wearing it or not. I particularly like it when I'm still in the piece of clothing she wants.

Kenneth, 32, duplicating service

Gina likes to wear any article of clothing that smells like me. She likes to smell me all over her. It's really a big thing to her. In fact, sometimes when we make love, she purposefully won't shower for the entire day so she can enjoy the aroma. It turns me on like a switch just thinking about it. Women are such sensual, gorgeous creatures.

Jon, 41, drug store clerk

25 Forbidden Sex

1. ***What do you consider the most forbidden form of sex?***
2. ***What forbidden sex act have you heard about a friend performing?***
3. ***Have you ever performed a sexual act that you consider forbidden?***
4. ***Have you ever cheated on your lover?***
5. ***Have you ever cheated with a younger woman?***
6. ***Have you ever left your wife or girlfriend for a younger woman? If so, did you ever return to your wife or girlfriend?***
7. ***Do women cheat as much as men do?***
8. ***Can a woman ever really get past the fact that her man cheated? Does it change things forever even if she says she forgives him? Describe.***

1. What do you consider the most forbidden form of sex?

Anal sex. That is too carnal for my taste.

Rob, 23, fry cook

Adultery. There's no excuse for it. If she doesn't want to be with me, I'll gladly let her go. If I don't want to be with her, I'll leave. That's the way it should be. You know, they use to hang adulterers.

Bryon, 28, auto sales

Forbidden sex is probably anything that feels just a little bit too good.

Timothy, 32, water department engineer

If the thought of doing it makes the hair on the back of my neck stand up, or if the idea makes me harder than I've been in years, I know it must be forbidden sex.

Herman, 43, weather forecaster

If they have a special file folder for the subject on the Internet, and you need a password to get in, then that is my definition of forbidden sex.

Geoff, 27, web site designer

Forbidden sex is not having permission. Without consent, any type of sex with anyone is rape. In addition to that, to bed a woman that men can clearly see has had too much to drink is in the rape category, also. How small does a man have to be to take advantage of a woman? Say, about the size of a gnat?

Duwayne, 36, hotel management

2. What forbidden sex act have you heard about a friend performing?

A friend told me about the time he let a guy perform oral sex on him. He swears it was the best blow job he ever had, and supposedly, it was the only time he let it happen. I don't know whether to believe him or not. He's such a liar.

Joey, 24, waiter

I know this guy who did it with five hookers at one time. I thought he was bragging and joking around. He was hell-bent on proving it to me, so he called the escort service up again and invited me to join the next round. The cost was outrageous, but so was the pleasure level. We're both very married guys, and therefore that was definitely forbidden sex. It was a great way to spend his income tax refund, but we'll probably go to hell for it.

Harold, 46, office supply store owner

I used to have an interesting friend, but I'm not allowed to associate with him anymore. Having said that, I'll tell you why. He is so "out there" with his sexual permissiveness it amazes even me. Hookers would be old-fashioned to him, that's not exciting enough. He has to have female *and* male hookers. The weirdest part of it to me is that he doesn't actually have sex with any of them. He looks. He watches them. He invites men and women to his home, locks all the doors, and the party begins. While they have sex with each other, he sits in the middle of the room, candles burning dimly, low music playing in the background, with a bowl of fruit and a bottle of expensive wine. They all know what the requirements are before they come (no pun intended). They know up front that they will be having sex with each other instead of with the "john." All the "prostitutes for hire" seem to wildly enjoy it. Not as much as Henry does, of course. No one could enjoy this as much as Henry. As he sits in the glow of the room watching these people have sex with each other, he sips his wine, eats his bananas and strawberries with a fixed smile of satisfaction on his face. Finally, when it would appear he can't contain himself any longer—he masturbates himself and cums in the empty fruit bowl, sips the finals of his wine as they are dressing and departing, then tucks himself into bed for a good night's slumber. Now that's my idea of weird. My wife has a slightly stronger opinion of Henry. She thinks he should be shot.

Henry's friend Joe, 43, police officer

3. Have you ever performed a sexual act that you consider forbidden?

Sex with three other people. I don't like group sex. I was very drunk. I sincerely believe that sex should only be between two people. I have not gotten drunk since that night.

Calvin, 24, waiter

Sex with an animal and sex with a plastic doll are no-nos. Anything else is a go.

Vance, 19, student

No. There is no such thing among adults.

Adam, 34, sound and lighting engineer

I used to have fantasies about my baby-sitter when I was in eighth grade, but I never did anything. Then I moved on to bigger and better things when my girlfriend's mother came on to me when I was in college. I thought *The Graduate* was make-believe—just a writer writing a great movie—until I met Gloria. I couldn't believe what was happening, but I sure went along for the ride to find out what was next. In the final analysis, having Gloria and her daughter Jennifer at the same time was enjoyable physically, but a wee bit more than I could cope with.

Mark, 36, accountant

4. Have you ever cheated on your lover?

It is sad to say, but I do it all the time. My wife is not a sexual creature. I simply have to have sex three to four times a week. I get it from my wife once a week if she feels up to it. I need it more than that.

Peter, 42, gas station owner

No. I've thought about it, I've been tempted, I've been asked and even been given reason to do it. I just couldn't do that to my wife or myself.

Roger, 36, carpenter

Every time I screw around on my wife, she gets a new outfit. She's happy, I'm happy. Big deal. It's a small price to pay for easing my Catholic guilt.

James, 40, club owner

Guys like that should be squeezed from society like pus from a pimple. They make it hard on the good guys when we've got a healthy and respectable hard-on. Women tend to be afraid of all of us because of those assholes.

James, 30, telephone repairman

5. Have you ever cheated with a younger woman?

Before I was married I had a great relationship with this younger girl. She was of legal age, but just barely. As it turned out, all we had going was fun and lusty sex. It ended when I asked my wife to marry me. I miss her sometimes, but I love my wife.

Terry, 46, factory maintenance

Not "robbing the cradle" younger. Nothing illegal. But, yes, with a younger woman who was quite a bit younger than myself. It was great and it was bad. We had nothing to discuss, but the fucking was off the charts.

Nathan, 42, insurance representative

Well, duh! Why would anybody cheat with an older woman? You can get that at home.

Ray, 46, bondsman

I went through a time in life where I had something to prove. I was on a selfish, ego-induced mission. Young women with sleek legs and simple, uneducated minds were my specialty. Then I grew up, fortunately, and learned the hard way how enjoyable a grown woman can be. The companionship and quality time spent with my girlfriend is much more fulfilling. I no longer have to explain who Bob Seger is.

Alan, 45, beauty salon owner

6. Have you ever left your wife or girlfriend for a younger woman? If so, did you ever return to your wife or girlfriend?

I would never leave my wife for anyone else, much less a younger woman. We have been together for thirty-five years. I still love and want her just as much as the day we got married.

Reggie, 55, pilot

Yes and no. I became completely insecure and brain-dead when I hit forty. I found myself with a young, vivacious woman of twenty-five. The sex was hot and she was always ready. The end of the story was very unlike television. I was filled with guilt, we had nothing in common other than sex, and my wife laughed when I tried to go home. I miss my wife, my children, and my home. If that's not bad enough, even our friends cut me off. I feel like a fool.

Lawrence, 47, lawyer

I did the opposite. I married a much younger girl and then left her for a woman my own age. I didn't have twenty extra years to wait for my cute, little wife to grow up.

Clay, 46, union representative

I'd like to go home, but I know it would never be the same and I'd continually be punished. And if she didn't continually punish me, I'd punish myself and not be able to relax—ever. I know it wouldn't work. My wife didn't deserve the treatment she received from me. I never deserved my wife. Well, now that I have destroyed everything and carried out this self-fulfilling prophecy, I guess I can go drown myself. Just kidding. It just sounds so depressing when I put it in words. Men should appreciate the woman they have, not be so self-serving, learn patience, take care of their families and children, and most important—handcuff their dick to their bedpost until they grow up.

Ernie, 37, locksmith

7. Do women cheat as much as men do?

If a woman is not happy at home, yes, she is just as likely to cheat. They are more discreet and don't get caught as often as men do. They seem to fall in love more often with the person they are cheating with.

Edward, 29, dental assistant

I want to meet that woman. I am not ready for a commitment. I want to get laid every now and then. Tell me where I can find one.

Kelly, 19, waiter

No, or at least they are better at it and don't get caught as often.

Wallace, 51, engineer

Hell, no, they don't cheat as much. They're not as afraid or as stupid. Men cheat for two reasons: guilt and fear. Then they have more guilt and more fear. It's a dumb and dumber and dumbest contest with themselves.

Woodrow, 51, hotel manager

If you believe the reports, there must be this one superslut out there fucking about eight thousand men a day, because no woman I know ever admits to screwing around. Just who is it all these guys are poking in the night if it isn't some other guys' wives?

Bill, 30, florist

8. Can a woman ever really get past the fact that her man cheated? Does it change things forever even if she says she forgives him? Describe.

A woman can forgive a man for cheating, but I don't know any who can completely forget and trust a man after he has done the dirty deed with someone else. I sure wouldn't forgive *her.*

Judd, 38, airline mechanic

Now, here's a subject for some musing. Women try to forget and women are pretty good at forgiving. They make it through as much as can be expected. Completely get past it? That's impracticable. If men could feel the heartaches they cause women, maybe they'd slow up. It's self-sabotage, as well, for a man to engage in sexual subterfuge.

George, 55, banker

Sure, it changes things forever. If women could forgive divinely, they would be angelic and not of this world any more than you or me.

Palmer, 59, retired

If she wants to get over it, she can. Women give birth. They can get over anything!

Felix, 51, sanitation engineer

You bet it changes things. Forever and ever and ever. The wedding vows of love and evil deception do not go hand in hand. Men are crazy to think women can get over it. They're jerks, just selfish jerks.

Tim, 31, musician

26 What If . . .

1. ***If money were no object, what sexual fantasy would you like to experience?***
2. ***Pretend you are a woman. What kind of man would turn you on?***
3. ***If you were a woman for a week, what would you do different from your mate?***
4. ***What would you like to do sexually if you were a woman for one week?***
5. ***If you could go anywhere in the world with your lover for a love fest, where would it be and how would you travel?***
6. ***If your mate could pretend you were her mystery lover, what do you think she would do differently?***
7. ***What if you could have any job in the world. What would you choose?***
8. ***If you could live anywhere, where would it be and why?***
9. ***If you were wealthy, what would you do with your money? Would you work anyway? If not, what would you do with your time?***

10. **If you could have any woman, whom would you choose?**
11. **If you could sexually start all over, how would you do things differently?**

1. If money were no object, what sexual fantasy would you like to experience?

I would go to a private island and have a harem of barely legal girls. I would make them wait on my every whim instead of always taking care of their needs and demands.

Thomas, 37, banker

A room in Las Vegas full of beautiful, wild women, an endless fountain of liquor and food, and the stamina to keep up. Something tells me the latter might be the hitch.

Peter, 50, marketing specialist

I'd like to have sex with famous women. I know they probably aren't any better in bed than the girl next door, but the bragging rights would be so great. Who cares about the girl next door? I want to fuck a dozen movie stars and tell everyone I know how it felt. I would kiss and tell my ass off.

Eugene, 20, video store clerk

I'd hire a governess first. Someone really experienced in child care to move in and take care of the children. My wife would never enjoy anything away from home unless the children were in good hands. Grandparents couldn't handle the length of time I'd like to spend in private with Nancy. Then I'd buy a yacht and fill it with the best staff money could hire and set sail with my wife. We'd stay gone at least two months. I'd take the best food, the best music, and all the comforts she likes. Passionate love-making while listening to the sounds of the sea—never having to fix a meal or wash a dish—what better dream than this? Just my beautiful Nancy and me. One of these days . . .

Vince, 47, CPA

2. Pretend you are a woman. What kind of man would turn you on?

A man that knows what I want before I can say it. One that would give me fabulous sex every night or day without hesitation. One who was beside me, interested in all the things I do. A man that would be there for only me, not Mom, work, or anyone else.

David, 26, telemarketer

Hardheaded men have their place and would with me if I were a woman. The right head needs to be hard. We're talking penis here. I would want a sexually active and lusty man, a firm body, strong legs, and very large hands that could bring me to my knees with one touch. He would have body hair like a monkey and he would be tall and powerful. Now, on the inside, here's the challenge: sensitive, sharing, kind, tender, gentle—am I making you sick yet? I would insist he be honorable, witty, smart, and have a sense of humor to last a lifetime—and the insight to see through a crisis and discover the real issues. He would be my stud and my leader.

Steven, 39, social worker

You know the answer! A guy just like me, because I am simple perfection. I'd fuck me in a New York minute.

Bradley, 26, gym instructor

A sex god in a suit of character.

Howard, 38, manufacturing company

3. If you were a woman for a week, what would you do different from your mate?

I would try to please my man a little bit better without all the whining and complaining. I would understand that he works hard all day long. When he gets home, I'd realize that he needs a little time to unwind. I would support him in all things that benefit us as a couple.

Rod, 35, carpenter

I would be more energetic about spreading my legs. I wouldn't try to break his bank account. I would be a slut for my man.

Eric, 24, carpenter

Shut my mouth.

Sean, 29, painter

If I was my wife, I'd suck my cock every possible moment. I'd beg for the opportunity to drink sperm and coat my face with the creamy stuff. And I'd pay very dearly for the priviledge. (I'm dreaming, right?)

Kenny, 32, nurse

Get rid of that fishy smell that permeates our bedroom from time to time. I never liked fishing and I certainly don't like to smell fish in bed while I'm trying to make love to my wife.

Stanley, 39, acoustical engineer

4. What would you like to do sexually if you were a woman for one week?

I would make all men fall at my feet whenever I walked by. I would throw temper tantrums exactly the way women do when they don't get their way.

Shane, 27, heavy equipment operator

I would seduce every man I came across. I would tease them. I would make them beg for fulfillment, then I would walk away.

Ryan, 32, park ranger

Well, it wouldn't be a blow job, that's for sure. I'd like to see what sex feels like from a woman's point. I'd take lots of notes and learn everything I could while I had the chance, in hopes it would make me a better lover.

Steve, 26, luggage sales

I can't imagine why it takes a woman so much longer than a man to come to an orgasm. My girlfriend takes an hour or more. Maybe it's just indicative of how terrible I am at pleasing her. I'd like to walk that hour in her panties to find out what I should be doing.

Mark, 22, fast-food worker

5. If you could go anywhere in the world with your lover for a love fest, where would it be and how would you travel?

I would go to a remote mountain cabin. No phones, television, or computers. We would fly away in a hot-air balloon and spend most of the time getting to know each other all over again. I love my wife, but we are both busy with work and kids. We need to discover the joys of being with each other again.

Bart, 45, bank vice president

Somewhere warm and breezy by the ocean. We would make love, eat, sleep, and start all over again. Life is hard and very fast-paced. I would love the chance to romance my wife afresh. How we would get there is of no importance to me.

Martin, 47, law enforcement officer

Since we are just having fun here, I'd like to go around the world on a flying carpet. It would naturally have a built-in Jacuzzi, killer sound system, and custom minibar.

Ross, 30, data processor

I'd like to go out West on a Harley, with my babe strapped on behind me. Her firm breasts would be poking me in my back, and her warm tongue would lick my ear all the way.

Henry, 25, soundman

We would board a plane to New York City. Both of us love Broadway plays and exotic restaurants. We would hide out in a fancy hotel with enough bubble bath and sex gadgets to fill an entire suitcase alone. I'd buy her new clothes and wine and dine her all over New York.

Ross, 35, truck driver

6. If your mate could pretend you were her mystery lover, what do you think she would do differently?

She would want me to love her for her mind and body. She is always telling me I only want sex from her. She would want me to cuddle and kiss and give her lots of foreplay.

Lawrence, 19, short order cook

If I were her mystery lover, she would probably love it. She could pull all her lame tricks on me, like she did when we first met. I'd believe it when she told me that giving her oral sex always cured her headaches. I'd respect her "religious" beliefs to not have anal sex. Now I know she was just full of excuses. Her mystery lover wouldn't have a clue.

Barry, 34, merchandiser

She'd take pictures and videos. Hot, sexy photos of me doing all the things she loves best. I'm quite a stud, you know.

Ralph, 42, oceanographer

My wife would love to talk trash. She's so shy I think it's painful for her some of the time. Like there's a screaming whore in her that wants so badly to get out. She was raised to be refined, but I know that trash-talking hot thing inside her will win one of these days and she'll love it.

Terry, 39, taxi driver

7. What if you could have any job in the world. What would you choose?

I would be a professional stud puppy. I would make women fall all over me and want me for my body. I would just lie there and let them have their way and get paid for it.

Josh, 21, singer

I'd take it. Any job that pays well and has benefits, I'd take it. I've been unemployed for about two years. Money is tight and our love life has greatly suffered.

Owen, 45, former commercial photographer

I'd like to be the guy who trims women's pubic hair for all those centerfold photos. That would be worth getting out of bed for each day.

Clint, 19, struggling student

Can you be a professional lotto winner? Not a player, but a winner? I'd do that job with a smile.

Hank, 24, pizza maker

The job I'm most happy doing is being a love slave for my wife. I'm already her love slave, her house slave, her slave, period. It's just that I don't get paid for it. If I could get paid for that, I'd have it made.

J.D., 28, hotel chef

8. If you could live anywhere, where would it be and why?

I would live in my own world where I was the ruler. Everyone would be at my beck and call. I'm tired of everyone telling me what to do and where to go and how to do it.

Peter, 45, pharmacist

I'd live between my baby's silky thighs. The view is great and I'd never be thirsty.

Keith, 24, furniture maker

Anywhere my girlfriend lives is where I want to be. She is going to be a big star someday, and I'm going to be her manager. She has the looks. I have the smarts, and a promise to break her face if she trys to screw me over.

Spencer, 20, talent agent

Inside my woman's vagina, with the warmth of those lips around my entire body day and night.

Stu, 25, tire manufacturer

9. If you were wealthy, what would you do with your money? Would you work anyway? If not, what would you do with your time?

I would work. I am not one who can stay at home and do nothing. I could never find enough things to do to fill my time. After a while boating, skiing, womanizing, and other leisures would get boring.

Tony, 32, restaurant manager

Hell, no, I wouldn't work. Not in the traditional sense, anyway. I'd learn to play the piano, improve my golf, and learn to romance my wife all over again. Just maybe I'd get it right this time.

Jack, 40, radio executive

I'd have fun with my money. I'd play and bring my true friends along with me. If I were as smart as I hope, my money would make more money for me just from wise investments. So the more I spend, the more I make. I like the sound of it.

Cal, 23, financial trainee

I'd buy the prettiest pussy money can provide. I'd have a new beauty every day. They'd receive a million bucks for each night they spent with me, so I'd have the world's most desirable women waiting in line for the privilege of making me happy. I'd dangle another million dollars in front of them as a bonus. Talk about incentive!

Perry, 29, broadcast technician

I would definitely work for fear that I would become a couch potato if I didn't. If I were wealthy, I'd surely have myself encircled by beautiful women. Women like money and rightfully so. What girl in her right mind wouldn't? With lots of money a guy can take a girl on a continuous flight of fancy. No scrubbing toilets, no dirty diapers, teenagers holding out their hands for the keys to your car—that kind of stuff would bite the dust. I'd pamper her until she had everything her heart desired and then start from the beginning. The best part would be having the freedom to take a flight to the south of France on a whim, eat dinner, make love without any interruptions, and return home.

Todd, 41, stockbroker

10. If you could have any woman, whom would you choose?

I would choose my wife all over again. I love her that much. I will always love her and I knew that the day I met her. It was love at first sight. Honestly.

Thomas, 82, retired

I would choose a blonde who has an hourglass figure and no brains. I would be the envy of all men. She would be eager to please only me of course. She has to be good in bed or I'd discard her like the wind.

Hugh, 19, minimart clerk

I'd make love to the current beauty queen from every nation in the world. That way I'd have the best of every culture, color, and nationality. I'd learn all the international secrets. I'd be tired, but very educated by the time I was through.

Simon, 42, travel agent

My high school sweetheart, who died in an automobile accident when we were just freshmen. I loved that girl more than anything, and still do. It has been the one big stumbling block in my life.

Terry, 30, health club owner

Assuming I could first get away from my wife for more than forty-five minutes, I would choose a woman who was mute. I love my wife, but those lips never seem to stop moving, and she's not whispering "sweet nothings" in my ear, either.

Billy, 48, water company

Goldie Hawn absolutely floats my boat like no other woman alive. That smile! Her personality! What a zesty, fun woman she must be to live with. Great looking. Cheerful and happy. Perfectly yummy! I would crawl on my hands and knees across a bed of nails to get to that woman's feet and be her slave.

Ned, 40, stockbroker

11. If you could sexually start all over, how would you do things differently?

I would do several things differently. First, I would be more open to my girl. Second, I would be more thoughtful of her feelings and needs. Last, I would ask her to marry me. I lost my chance several years ago and I still regret it. I am very sorry I let her get away.

Johnny, 40, army captain

I'd start by having some respect for women in general. Then, I would have more self-respect. Having improved on those two traits, I'd have an easier life with a much better sense of what's important. Men, me included, grow up laughing about our selfishness, womanizing, partying, and treating women with little or no respect whatsoever. We need to get back to the real values.

Todd, 35, estate planner

I wouldn't wait so long to get started. I would focus on having great sex with the prettiest women who would talk to me. I would not waste so much time on developing "relationships" with ugly women.

Gilbert, 27, computer repairman

Trish and I loved each other in high school, and we still love each other. If I had the chance, I would not marry so young. We would probably still have married, but not before college. She worked so hard to get me through law school, I ached in my heart for her. There wasn't anything we could do to change our schedule, but if I had it to do over again, we would have dated until I was out of school and firmly on my feet with my career. Getting married and having a baby and going to law school was really hard on us.

Larry, 45, lawyer

27 Safe Sex

1. ***Has the AIDS epidemic changed your sexual habits? How?***
2. ***How important do you think it is to practice safe sex?***
3. ***How much of your partner's sexual history do you like to know before you engage in intercourse?***
4. ***Do you practice safe sex? All the time?***
5. ***How do you practice safe sex?***
6. ***What do you consider to be the safest form of sex?***
7. ***Have you ever had phone sex?***
8. ***Have you ever had cybersex?***
9. ***Have you ever thought your lover was healthy only to find out later that she wasn't? If so, did she know she wasn't healthy and conceal it from you intentionally?***
10. ***Do you ejaculate outside of your partner, but in her presence, to practice safe sex?***

1. Has the AIDS epidemic changed your sexual habits? How?

Surely you jest. Of course it has changed the way I am sexually. I don't want to die for a piece of ass. I am very careful about the people I sleep with. I have to really know the person and trust her totally. I always have protected sex.

Jacob, 34, sales

It has not changed my sex life in any way. I am happily married. She was a virgin when we were married. I only have sex with her.

Howard, 47, pilot

I used to swing. Now I don't. I used to pick up strange women at bars. Now I don't. I used to have casual sex with men. Now I don't even think about it. I used to have a great time. Now I watch a lot of videos and beat off in motel rooms.

Chris, 43, industrial sales rep

Yes, it's made me keep my zipper shut more times than I care to mention.

Vincent, 28, government employee

While living in SoHo, I was dating this gorgeous gal named Becky. She worked for a law firm and I was in medical school. We had the perfect life. Both of us young, attractive, and successful; we thought we had the world by the tail until one night I'm sitting there looking at her across the table during a romantic dinner for two, and she says to me, "Paul, I have to be checked for AIDS, and so do you." I felt as if I would fall into my soup. I had my first out-of-body experience right then and there. An old boyfriend of hers, from years ago, came up positive. He wasn't gay. He just showed up with AIDS, just like that. He didn't have a clue as to where and when he became a carrier, and there we are talking about us possibly having the same thing. It was just too weird. I don't think I've ever been more frightened in my entire life. As it turned out, neither of us carried the virus, but it sure made me look differently at the possibilities of normal heterosexual people contracting this horrible disease. Becky and I got married about six months later and we're still together. I have been the most monogamous husband you will ever meet.

Paul, 41, doctor

2. How important do you think it is to practice safe sex?

I don't care one way or another because I only have sex with my wife and have for thirty years. I trust her completely. What the other people do with their lives is their own business.

Borace, 75, retired

Safe is the only way to have sex with me. I hate the condoms, but love the sex. I want to live for a long time to come.

Edwin, 26, forest-fire fighter

Life or death. That's fairly substantial to me.

Leith, 30, professional gardener

Everyone talks so big about always having safe sex, but I know for a fact that it isn't always that way. If I can talk my way into some girl's pants and she is all hot and bothered, she is going to fuck me. She might want me to use a rubber, but she isn't going to push me away if I don't have one. I know this is true. Horny teenagers fuck first and worry about the consequences later. Why do you think all these girls have all these little crying babies hanging on their ankles?

Tyler, 19, checkout clerk

It's like bubbles for Lawrence Welk. I can't imagine sex without safety.

Jim, 47, dating service

3. How much of your partner's sexual history do you like to know before you engage in intercourse?

I would like to know every man she has been intimate with, but that's highly unlikely. I have to be comfortable with her and her past. Then I basically go on a trust basis. I guess it is kinda stupid.

Bart, 25, lab technician

None. I don't want to know any of it. I have safe sex. As long as I'm protected, I don't want to know if I measure up to their performance.

Benton, 32, phlebotomist

If I am hard and she is wet, that's all I need to know.

Walter, 20, T-shirt printer

I like to know what she learned from her experiences.

Pete, 45, genealogist

I used to worry about normal things—will she be a good mother for my children? Does she have a crazy ex-husband? Is she a good person, friendly, attractive, etc. Now I worry about *everything.* Where has she been and with whom? It's a mind-blowing experience to date these days. It's hard on everyone. It's impossible to know what you're getting into. People lie. People tell the truth. The problem is worse than deciding who is telling the truth and who is lying. Do they really know? I have heard rumors of women who thought they were healthy and they weren't. I want to see their health card, and often. I sleep with no one who doesn't have a clean bill of health and a current health card to prove it. Sorry. No exceptions.

Sam, 38, government employee

4. Do you practice safe sex? All the time?

That is the only way to get in my pants. I take enough chances with my job.

Jed, 24, coal miner

I start out that way, always—every time. I think about it, I ask questions about her sexual habits, her health, etc. I use a condom the first time and then, never again with that person. I don't know why. Maybe it's the intimacy. Maybe it's trust. Maybe it's just crazy.

Norman, 50, radio producer

I would like to say I do, but I don't. Since my divorce from my wife of ten years, I have made plenty of judgment calls based on the working status, physical appearance, and cleanliness of the woman I was dating. I'm now beginning to understand what a mistake that is. You can't tell anything by that kind of measurement. Condoms just aren't my cup of tea. I hate them—those damn plastic penis holders. It's almost enough to make me want to give up sex when I think about having to use condoms in order to be safe. I'll have to think of something else. Cards claiming a clean bill of health, I suppose.

Malcome, 44, electrician

5. How do you practice safe sex?

The only way to practice safe sex is to wait until I get married. Yes, I am still a virgin. I know that is unheard of nowadays, but I'm a true virgin. I am damn proud of it.

Randy, 18, student

I wear a raincoat.

Bud, 39, X-ray technician

I let my girlfriend unroll a condom on my erection with her warm mouth. She pops it in and goes real slow down my shaft. She has become quite talented with her skill. I'd like to show her abilities off to the guys, but I don't think I could ever talk her into it. She'd probably just bite my prick to prove her point.

Terry, 28, commercial glass installer

Over and over and over again, until it's permanently in your brain and you do it like brushing your teeth.

William, 40, restaurant owner

No glove, no love.

Bill, 26, lawn specialist

6. What do you consider to be the safest form of sex?

Abstinence. Period. That is the only form of true safe sex.

Ralph, 28, steel-factory worker

Zip. But who is going to adhere to that? Other than no sex, the key has got to be using protection every single time and knowing as much as you possibly can about your partner. It takes the spontaneity out of sex and passion, but you're alive to tell everyone how boring it is.

Gregory, 36, automotive repair shop owner

Going without. Now, what are the possibilities of that happening? I couldn't help but laugh at this question. Ha, ha. I'm not going to do without, so I have to carry condoms with me at all times. I also laugh when I getting ready to throw up. It relieves the tension of the moment, I suppose.

Jesse, 25, retail sales

7. Have you ever had phone sex?

Is there really such a thing?

Terrell, 56, pilot

My wife and I have phone sex all the time. I travel in my line of work. While I am in the hotel, we have great sex over the phone. We talk dirty and masturbate. At times I want to reach out and touch her, it seems so real.

Abel, 43, stockbroker

My girl goes to school in another state, and phone sex is about all we have. When we see each other on breaks, it takes a while for us to get used to the fact that we are actually in the same room. We are shy, awkward, and a little inhibited until we get over the overwhelming sensations of being able to touch, taste, and smell each other. I feel like I'm with a stranger sometimes.

Dana, 22, law student

Heavens to betsy, no. I don't even *know* how people have sex over the phone. What an impersonal thing that must be.

Randall, 51, retail buyer

8. Have you ever had cybersex?

What is that? I can honestly say that the only form of sex I've had is in bed with my wife.

Joshua, 38, tree trimmer

Yes. It's not much, but it's better than nothing, and it's safe sex, for certain. There was this one lady that had a wonderful imagination and she led me down a path of ecstasy like I have never experienced. If I could ever talk her into meeting me, I'd probably marry her.

Frank, 39, optician

It costs so much per minute on-line, I can't enjoy myself. I like to look at all the dirty pictures on the Web, but I'm always aware that the clock is ticking, and my money is flying away. If I rush, I can't enjoy myself. And if I take my time, I can't afford it.

Pat, 45, furniture refinisher

Cybersex, now there's a thought. Imagine Julius Caesar having cybersex with Cleopatra. I know we're living in the nineties, on the fast track, the digital everything, the superelectronichighway, high-techno days, but cybersex just doesn't do it for me. I cannot comprehend cybersex.

Charles, 55, utility company

9. Have you ever thought your lover was healthy only to find out later that she wasn't? If so, did she know she wasn't healthy and conceal it from you intentionally?

The only person I would not trust is a hooker. I would not believe that she is healthy. But I am not that desperate, thank God.

Maurice, 24, housepainter

I dated a woman who lied about her name, her age, her marital status, and her job. If the bitch gave me something fatal, I'll spend my dying days hunting her down.

Eric, 30, bartender

My wife knew she had breast cancer a year before she told me. She thought I'd leave her if I knew how sick she was. I feel cheated that our last months together weren't spent making her as happy as she could have been. She hid the severity of her illness until it was too late to do much to help her.

Paul, 47, car salesman

I'd kill her. I don't think anyone in their right mind would do that, and if they did, they would be better off not dating me.

Chad, 23, student

Yes, this happened to me. I was dating an intelligent woman in her forties. You would think an intelligent woman wouldn't date anyone without practicing safe sex, but she did. She didn't use condoms and I came to find out that she had dated many, many men. I didn't know that, either, until later. She scared me out of my mind and I hated her for that. Needless to say, we stopped dating immediately. I'm lucky I'm not dead. I hope there's a special place in hell for people that don't practice safe sex.

Bobby, 49, computer repairman

10. Do you ejaculate outside of your partner, but in her presence, to practice safe sex?

My lover enjoys letting me masturbate onto her belly. She says it's a turn-on the way I firmly hold my penis as I stroke myself to a climax. This is not for safe sex purposes. We just like to do it to please ourselves when the other is not up to having intercourse.

Pat, 32, roofer

Never to practice safe sex, but often because it's great fun. It's erotic to come all over my baby's breasts and see the physical expression of passion.

Kevin, 34, home improvement business

No, I use those tacky little rubber things I hate.

Kyle, 21, student

I sure do. I also use condoms and she uses creams. Between the two of us, we have enough safe-sex toys and equipment to keep us busy. I think we spend more time being safe than the average person, but that's okay. We'll stay alive and healthy. Somebody has to stay around to bury all those idiots.

Quinton, 20, student and newspaper reporter

28 Male Mystique & Myth-Understandings

1. ***What are men most secretive about, and why?***
2. ***What do you think about helping women with household chores?***
3. ***Do you share household chores with your mate? Do you divide them equally?***
4. ***Do you help with the children?***
5. ***Do you think women are smarter than men?***
6. ***Is it true—no matter how great the woman, men must have sexual variety?***
7. ***Do you think men exaggerate on issues of sex and cheating?***
8. ***Do you understand men? The male ego?***
9. ***Why do you think some women believe men are animals?***
10. ***What should women know about men that would improve their relationships with them?***
11. ***What would you like to know about men if you were a woman?***
12. ***Is it true men think poorly of women who are sexually aggressive, but it's okay for men to be that?***
13. ***What's the one thing no man wants his woman to know?***

1. What are men most secretive about, and why?

I feel that men are most secretive about what they really want in bed. They are afraid that if they told them, women would have something to hold over them or would use the information to make them appear weak.

Kevin, 38, columnist

Men are afraid to let their girlfriends know the truth about their bank accounts, tax returns, and paychecks. When it comes to a man's money, the less a woman knows about it, the better.

Harvey, 50, home builder

Men will not admit the real size of their penises. They even make custom rulers that take six inches and make them appear to measure a foot. Only a guy would invent something like that, and you know only another guy would ever buy one.

Parker, 35, fishing guide

The precious little penis—when and where it's been. Especially if it *is* indeed little.

Bob, 50, marketing strategist

Men lie. They lie about women, they lie to women and for women. If they're intelligent, they cover that up. If they're not, they lie some more or they get screwed. Of course if what they're lying about is screwing someone they shouldn't be screwing, well, then, they deserve what they get.

Patrick, 31, sales

What I protect most is me. My fear, my vulnerability. Getting really close to a woman, letting her know my fears and disappointments, scares me. I reckon it's the inevitable little boy in me that just can't commit to fully trusting a woman.

Howard, 53, postal service

2. What do you think about helping women with household chores?

It depends on whether or not the woman works outside of the home. If she does, then, yes, I will help her in any way I can. If not, she better get off her lazy ass and keep the house clean.

Bill, 26, lumberyard operator

I think if I can get out of it, that's great. Often I play stupid, like I don't know how and would probably mess it up, anyway. She buys it sometimes and doesn't buy it most of the time. If I absolutely have to, I'll help, but believe me, I don't like it. Then again, I guess no one likes cleaning a toilet. Unless they are making forty-five dollars an hour doing it.

Dwight, 29, plumber

Even though no one likes to do housework, it's a necessity that won't go away, and I can't imagine the woman who puts up with a lazy, selfish man. I know they're out there, these martyr-type women, but how did they get that way? If their mothers were that way, you'd think they would be sick of watching lazy men get away with murder. She ought to let the laundry pile up and fill the house with the aroma of his dirty socks, until he finally wants to help. That's what I'd do.

Martin, 39, wholesale supply manager

3. Do you share household chores with your mate? Do you divide them equally?

I always try to help her, even though she'll redo things I just did. She says I don't know where to put stuff and that she can't find it later.

Ron, 43, real estate manager

I do all my housework. I live alone. I am not a slob as some men are. I can't stand dirt.

Rob, 43, bus driver

I make the mess. She cleans it up. That's my kind of sharing.

Howie, 23, bicycle mechanic

Equally? Probably not. I do help, but I'm sure I could do more. Frankly, it turns me on to watch my wife ironing my shirts with care and love. She is usually barefooted, standing there so soft and sweet looking, wearing only one of my old shirts. It usually provokes a passionate love session.

Sterling, 31, music store clerk

4. Do you help with the children?

I do not have children, but if we did, I would. I think I owe it to her and them to help out daily. If I helped make them, I should help raise them.

Ronnie, 24, tool sales

My help with the kids is the best part of my day. We read together, talk, take longs walks around the neighborhood, cook meals—we enjoy each other's company. I don't like the areas of discipline, but who does? I hate it when they fight, and I try my best to teach them to discuss their problems in a civilized manner. All in all, I love my kids.

Mitchell, 45, teacher

Oh, yeah. I help them pack their trunks for boarding school in the fall, and I give them Christmas presents in December. They are at camp all summer, and then we start all over again. I kind of like the precise nature of it all. It's a family tradition I firmly believe in.

Reggie, 47, investment banker

I definitely do. I help with everything—swim meets, track, baseball, cooking and cleaning, really a little bit of everything they're into. It's the music I can't stand. The Garbage People? Nine Inch Nails? I can't even understand the names, much less the music. But, I do try. I practically had nightmares the first time I saw a photo of Marilyn Manson.

Bill, 44, sawmill owner

5. Do you think women are smarter than men?

Not really. They just know how to use their brains differently than men do. Most men think with their dicks and not the heads on their shoulders.

Thorn, 38, machine operator

Women are always scheming something. That does not make them smarter. They are conniving pieces of slime. I'll take a man anytime.

Carl, 35, dancer

No, there are stupid people everywhere, regardless of gender.

J.D., 37, fisherman

Women are smarter in many ways. Men let their penises have way too much control.

Rueben, 26, counselor

6. Is it true—no matter how great the woman, men must have sexual variety?

No way. I have never had much variety in the sex department. I dated the same girl all through high school and college. We married my senior year. We are doing just fine without "variety." There are men who think that they have to have different stuff to stay happy; personally, I think they are not very mature or sure of themselves.

Dan, 45, professor

Unfortunately, it is. I'm one of those men. I don't think every man is this way, but most are unfaithful, deceitful—search endlessly for variety and shouldn't be trusted an inch. I've got a dick and always need somewhere to put it. I chase everything and get bored with everyone, eventually. Hell, I even bore myself.

Hal, 23, student

You don't eat the same meal every day. That pretty much says it all for me.

Bo, 30, housepainter

Not anymore it isn't. When heterosexual men started dying because of the AIDS virus, it got their attention. It used to be that nothing got their attention unless a woman had hold of their pecker. Not anymore.

Mitchell, industrial gas company

7. Do you think men exaggerate on issues of sex and cheating?

Of course we have to keep up our images as womanizers. I don't believe that half my friends have had the encounters they claim. But then I may be wrong and lead a boring life.

Ted, 26, bartender

Men are dogs in heat.

Lyle, 38, policeman

Who wants to admit that his wife is the only piece he gets to fuck? Have you seen most guys' women? For that matter, have you seen what most guys look like? We are a damn ugly bunch of breeders.

Sal, 35, plastics engineer

I hope so, otherwise I'm leading a very dull life and missing a lot. I know I need to get out more often and live it up, but work has me bogged down and busy. The men in my office talk about their escapades with women they meet and it gets me horny and frustrated. I think they exaggerate, and I've never been a cheating type, but it sure sounds good.

David, 37, accountant

Men exaggerate everything. The size of their dick, the size of their brain, and the size of their wallet. Mostly their little friend.

Barry, 40, office supply warehouse

8. Do you understand men? The male ego?

I don't understand the male ego or a woman's ego. I believe that there is a gene in our body that makes us act like simpering idiots when it comes to sex.

Ken, 21, lab research specialist

I understand what I need to know, if you know what I mean.

Jackie, 30, heat and cooling engineer

The male ego is the force that drives society. It is a great and powerful thing. Men should use it carefully.

Hank, 36, hunter

Of course I do. One word—fear.

William, 41, dentist

About as much as I understand rocket science.

Adam, 32, engineer

Yeah, they're pricks. That's one of the advantages of being a gay man: I don't have to deal with pricks.

Nicholas, 26, fashion industry

9. Why do you think some women believe men are animals?

Act like a duck and quack like a duck, must be a duck.

Tommy, 42, author

Because they are. Don't trust us. Especially if we say, "Trust me."

Danny, 41, salesman

Women think some men are animals because they have been led to believe all the things their mothers told them in childhood. It is kind of like how we are all afraid of snakes and bats and spiders, until we do a little research. Sometimes you find good in the strangest places.

Kerry, 35, veterinarian

There's a lot of us out here that appreciate a good woman. Then again, there's plenty of men that are nothing more than small children in large bodies—big swinging dick-types.

Duncan, 29, solvent company representative

10. What should women know about men that would improve their relationships with them?

I think they should know what leeches we are before they get attached to us and try to suck us dry.

Barry, 34, machine repairman

Don't be so quick to fall for a man. Know who you are and what you want in a relationship before you give your heart. Be independent and self-sufficient. Know that most men are snakes in the grass.

Dale, 27, graphic artist

Women should know that men don't really like to spend time with their own sisters, so why would they want to spend any time with yours?

Arthur, 36, radio announcer

If a guy hesitates to commit—dump him, he won't change. If a guy behaves selfishly, he *is* selfish and he won't change. I guess the message here is—men don't change. What you see is what you get. If you can be happy with that, fine. If it's not good enough in the first week, the first month or year, and you begin to see things that are unacceptable, it's time to leave. Bad men don't change. Good men don't change, either. They're either good or bad and all about choice. It's completely up to her which type of man a woman wants to spend her energy on.

Kevin, 41, photographer

11. What would you like to know about men if you were a woman?

What they really want out of life instead of what they say they want. It always seem to change as we get closer to each other.

Theo, 23, store clerk

Men are the same as women, but they don't want you to know it. What I would reveal to women is this: If you always remember that the closest thing to a man's heart is his dick, you can have anything your heart desires, and then some.

Kirk, 38, paint store owner

Probably not a damn thing. I'd get frustrated and go home.

Ricky, 29, graphic artist

12. Is it true men think poorly of women who are sexually aggressive, but it's okay for men to be that?

Give me an aggressive woman over a passive woman any day. They are the most exciting women to be in bed with. They will tell you what pleases them and seem to know what to do to please a man.

Allen, 45, liquor store owner

Men will bad-mouth an aggressive woman right up until the second she rips their underwear off with her teeth and plows into their wiggling worms.

George, 50, court officer

A secure man loves the attention of an aggressive woman.

Samuel, 61, community center director

This makes women sick, I know. They have desires just like men do, and men are clamoring all the time for women to give it up and be more uninhibited, when just about the time they relax, the men dog them and make them feel loose and whorish for admitting to their feelings. I feel terribly lucky if I just manage to get some occasionally.

Mike, 30, public notary

13. What's the one thing no man wants his woman to know?

I don't want any woman knowing how much money I have. I would be scared they only wanted me for that reason.

Bob, 49, pediatric doctor

How much he depends on her and her love. How much he is just a little boy in a man's body, trying to do the best he can and desperately needing her approval and acceptance.

Matthew, 44, jewelry business

That he squats when he pees.

Wylie, 53, diamond broker

His weakness. It's a cardinal sin to let a woman know your weakness.

Edward, 48, retail toy company

Men don't want women to know they need them. Insecurity keeps men from achieving true happiness with a woman. It sort of works for them, more than against them, however, in business. Competition is fierce and insecurity makes them work more arduously.

Jon David, 42, entrepreneur

29 Self

1. What do you think about jealousy? Have you ever been a jealous man?
2. Are you ever possessive?
3. What do you think about couch-potato-type men?
4. Are you a sports enthusiast or a sports fanatic?
5. Are you terribly romantic or terrible at trying to be romantic?
6. What do you want people to say about you when you're gone?
7. What kind of funeral do you want for yourself?
8. Are you an honorable man?
9. Is there ever a good reason to lie?
10. Is there a big difference beween a lie and a little white lie?
11. Do you have a good relationship with your mother?
12. If you could change anything about your mother, what would it be?

13. **Do you think your relationship with your mother has anything to do with your relationships with women? Or, more specifically, with the quality of your relationship with your mate?**
14. **Whom do you admire and why?**
15. **Do you keep many secrets from your woman?**
16. **For married men: How long have you been married and do you have a good marriage?**
17. **Where do you place the credit for having a good marriage or relationship?**
18. **If you have a troubled relationship with your mate, where do you place the blame?**
19. **For those who are intentionally not married, why are you not married?**
20. **What does commitment mean to you?**
21. **Is it easy for you to commit to a woman and your relationship with her?**
22. **If you have trouble committing, why do you?**
23. **Why is it important to the majority of women to have a committed, monogamous relationship with a man?**
24. **How do you feel about domestic abuse?**
25. **How do you feel about deadbeat dads?**
26. **Financial fears: If you have them, what are they and what do you believe causes them?**
27. **What personal achievement are you the most proud of?**
28. **What would you like to accomplish that you haven't?**

29. **What scares you?**
30. **Are you in touch with your so-called feminine side?**
31. **Do you express your fears, emotions, and desires openly with your mate?**
32. **What does being a man mean to you?**

1. What do you think about jealousy? Have you ever been a jealous man?

I am so busy with work and home life, I don't have time to be jealous.

Alan, 36, bank executive

I'm only jealous when we are in a public place and another man tries to come on to my girl as soon as I walk away from her, whether it's to go to the rest room or to get us drinks. She is a very sexy lady. At least she knows who she came with, and I know who she will leave with.

Bart, 29, bridal designer

I take my cue from the girl I'm with. If she ignores me or makes me feel unimportant, her actions and reactions to other men can make me jealous.

Adam, 24, swimming instructor

Been there, done that. It's the most considerable waste of time known to mankind. Women either want you or they don't. I'm lucky *and* deserving of my wife's love. Lucky in the beginning—now it's the effort on my part that is pulling the weight. Men can hold their heads high and be proud of themselves when they treat women well. Men who don't should be exiled to a far, far place.

Clifton, 47, computer programmer

2. *Are you ever possessive?*

All men are possessive by nature. It is an animal instinct, so, yes, I am to a degree. But not to the point that it will hurt my relationship.

Roy, 37, banker

The day I gave my dick to my wife, I took ownership of her pussy. Believe me, she got the better end of the deal, but, yes, I want what is rightfully mine.

Tim, 49, real estate agent

I still have the first comic book I ever bought. I never throw anything away. Am I possessive? Only of things I really care about. If I love her, I want to keep her.

Edward, 29, security alarm installer

I spent the first twenty years of my dating life being a possessive man. Over Diane, I got in fights, ended up with broken bones and, finally, a police record. My rap sheet looks like my grandmother's Thanksgiving grocery list. I'm not at all proud of it, and in being so stupid I lost Diane to a better man—at least a man more in control of his emotions and desires.

Harold, 45, furniture manufacturing

3. What do you think about couch-potato-type men?

I think they ought to get up off their dead ass and get a life. It's all too short as it is.

Calvin, 25, lifeguard

Honey, bring me a beer.

Lance, 36, butcher

I think their girlfriends should give them all a big bag of chips and a six-pack of beer. Then while their men are pigging out, the ladies need to get on over to my house for some good loving from a real man.

Cecil, 28, building crane operator

Leave them be. I like my couch and I only date women who like my couch.

Vernon, 49, painter

4. Are you a sports enthusiast or a sports fanatic?

Hey, I am man, hear me roar! Of course I like sports. I'm just not a fanatic about it. I mean, I do it for a living, but I'm not nuts.

Jesse, 34, football player

The only sport I like is chasing women around my apartment. What a workout when I catch them.

Stuart, 21, lawn gardener

The television is my best friend in the whole world. I guess that's sick, but everything else in my life causes me too much trouble. My girlfriends are all jealous of the time I watch sports and play poker, but it gives me pleasure and I guess I'll keep doing it. When the right woman comes along, I'll slow it down. How I'm ever going to find her, I just don't know.

Leon, 24, restaurant service industry

I'm a fanatic, I guess. According to my wife, I spend "entirely too much time staring at the damn tube." It arouses me when she gets angry, and I usually win in the end because she starts bringing the love toys into the living room to try and distract me. I especially like the glow-in-the-dark toy. She buries it in the tastiest places. Of course, then I have to go and find it.

Lee, 31, mechanic

5. Are you terribly romantic or terrible at trying to be romantic?

I can romance with the best of them. I am so smooth I can slip right through your hands. And if that is not bad enough, I can bullshit my way into a woman's life. So move over little dog 'cause big dog is movin' in.

Nick, 34, advertising sales

Twenty years ago I was a romantic. Now I'm too tired or maybe bored to try.

Ralph, 45, nursery owner

When I am at the start of a new relationship, I pull out all my tricks. Candy, presents, singing telegrams, you name it. I become a big bowl of mush. Then after getting to know her better, things go downhill. By the time I rip a fart in her company and don't even notice it, the sizzle is certainly over.

Trey, 40, roofer

When Betty and I first met, she said I was the most romantic guy she had ever known. It's true I used to do more things for her, like buy flowers and have them sent to her office, take her to spontaneous lunches in the park, and on occasion, bring home a feminine gift just because I love her. I think the humdrum of life and work has been somewhat a damper. It's unfortunate that people get so caught up in life that the little, but actually more important, things get left by the sidelines. I think I'll make a list and get some of those admirable talents of mine out of the romance closet and shake off the dust.

Mitch, 48, construction management

6. What do you want people to say about you when you're gone?

I want people to remember what I have done, not who I was or what I have left them. They will probably just say, "Poor SOB," and go about their daily lives as if I were never here.

Alvin, 58, retired

Not a darn thing. They've said more than enough since I've been here.

Thurston, 59, freelance artist

How about "Who was that strange little man and why did he scare my cat?"

Bruce, 26, promotions manager

7. What kind of funeral do you want for yourself?

Who says I'm going anywhere? I don't want a lot of crying when I leave this earth. I would want those who knew me to remember me as a good guy with a caring heart and then get on with their lives.

Shelby, 24, nurse

I plan to leave a little bit of cash to all the women I've ever loved. The only catch is that they all have to attend my funeral and sit side by side through the service without saying one bad thing about me or each other. If one of them hears another talk negatively and can prove it, she gets the disgruntled one's share. That should keep their mouths shut.

Farley, 52, service station owner

I want the funeral director to embalm my pecker in a perpetual erection. Hell, he can even cut it off and insert a few more go-between inches if he wants to. Then I want to have an open casket service with my proud boner sticking straight up

Otto, 47, machinist

I thought about skipping this question altogether. Then I decided I'd answer it anyway. If I could have anything I wanted at my funeral, it would be naked women and all of my buddies around to enjoy it and thank me. My wife broke up our Monday-night football, Wednesday-night bowling, and Friday-night poker, one little nag at a time.

Clarence, 51, contractor

8. Are you an honorable man?

If you are a true and honest man, then you have to have some kind of honor. Without honor, there is chaos and constant upheaval in one's life. Who needs that.

Creed, 39, personnel director

Honor is imperative to any human existence. Living without honor is living without. Existence is not living.

Patrick, 48, pediatric physician

There is honor among thieves. It doesn't say anything about men.

Rodney, 27, body shop worker

Honor: One who commands respect. A keen sense of ethical conduct. I presumably meet this to some degree or I wouldn't be with my wife. She is the most honorable person I have ever had the privilege of knowing.

Everett, 49, lawyer

9. Is there ever a good reason to lie?

I found out the hard way that there is never a good reason. It always comes back to haunt you, one way or another.

Jordan, 42, photo lab owner

When you lie, it will catch up with you, and then you'll have to lie again to cover up the first one. It is a vicious cycle that I can live without.

Burt, 35, land surveyor

I lie all the time, especially when it's convenient for me. It's easier than listening to all the bullshit.

Rodney, 44, builder

Only when I want there to be. Trouble, is I seem to need a good reason more often than I would like. My sweet Betty doesn't seem to know the difference, but it makes me feel more and more guilty. I guess I'm beginning to grow up.

John, 32, financial planner

Depends on who's getting their balls slammed in the wringer.

Steve, 21, student

10. Is there a big difference between a lie and a little white lie?

A lie is a lie. There is no excuse for either.

Joe, 59, semiretired

I wouldn't know, because I've been lying for one reason or another since I was eight or nine years old. It seems easier to lie than to listen to all the bitching and hell-raising I would get if I told the truth. I lie to protect myself.

Bart, 41, teacher

Lies made me the man I am today. I lied to get my first date with my wife. I lied when I told her I wasn't going to come, and I certainly lied when I told her I'd always be there for her.

Alexander, 38, blacksmith

If you have a really big penis, you should lie. If you have a little teenie tiny penis, you better lie.

Jerry, 26, computer technician

11. Do you have a good relationship with your mother?

Not always, it started out as a bad one. She was an alcoholic and never there for us kids. Thankfully she quit, and we are very close now. I would do anything for my mother. I can't say that for my so-called father.

Barney, 28, tree trimmer

My mother is the mother of all mothers. A just and good woman with a deep and kind soul. I wish I could be more like her and much less like my father. He's a jerk.

Tom, 41, musician

My parents are wonderful people. They are kind, caring, and generous. I only wish I hadn't caused them so much worry when I was a kid.

Mark, 24, salesman

I adore my mother. All mothers should be like mine and this world would be a better place. She's an angel.

Patrick, 23, student

12. If you could change anything about your mother, what would it be?

I would change the fact that she put up with so much horror and beatings from my father when I was too young to do anything about it. You better believe that as soon as I got big enough, he darn sure could not use her as his personal punching bag. I hate him to this day for the way he treated her. I'm just glad that he is dead and in a grave now.

Keith, 37, window washer

I'd make her richer and more willing to share her newfound wealth with her only son.

Andrew, 31, factory assembler

I'd make my mother be happier and better able to stop worrying and enjoy life more.

Cary, 25, potter

I'd start with her slut-looking wardrobe and work my way down to her big fat mouth, nosy nose, and uptight ass. My mother embarrasses me and drives me insane.

Alan, 25, graduate student

13. Do you think your relationship with your mother has anything to do with your relationships with women? Or, more specifically, with the quality of your relationship with your mate?

Of course, my mother taught her boys to respect and treat all women with the utmost care. If we didn't, we had hell to pay. I admire women for all that they put up with from men in general. My mother was a strong but loving mother and woman.

Bart, 45, layout designer

My mate is a man and I don't like women at all. Who knows if my mother has anything to do with that, but I doubt it. I just love men, that's all. I think the male body is beautiful and I like the company of men.

Marshall, 30, artist

I judge every woman based on the way my mother treated my father. If I can have anything close to what they had for fifty-two years of marriage, I will be a happy man.

Winston, 35, office worker

Everything revolves around a person's relationship with their family. From their genes to their attitudes on life in general, everything is nutured or crippled by their upbringing.

Xavier, 48, television industry

14. Whom do you admire and why?

I would have to say that I admire all the children that are trying to grow up in this world that we as adults have created for them. They have a rough world to change. It is not like it was when we were growing up. It is a hell of a lot tougher.

Kyle, 48, bank teller

I admire anyone who made it into the history books. Presidents, war heroes, inventors, writers, actors, scientists. One of the first disappointments I can remember in my lowered expectations for life was the moment I realized that I was never going to be president and most people won't know I ever lived on the face of this earth.

Harry, 32, college instructor

I admire my sons. They have learned from watching my mistakes and are making much better choices.

Gregory, 45, marine biologist

15. Do you keep many secrets from your woman?

If I have learned anything in my life, it is not to even try to keep secrets from my wife. She will always find them out. I haven't the foggiest idea how she does it either.

Willard, 39, grocery store owner

If I have a relationship such as the one I now have, I keep no secrets. The question is, How long will this one last? Just dating women, I keep many secrets. It's none of their business. I know I need to open up more, but I can't and probably won't until I'm married to my partner for life.

Fulton, 30, social worker

Lies made me what I am today, and secrets keep me alive and kicking.

Nolan, 42, dispatcher

I try, but she still seems to find out everything. It's that sixth sense about her I can't seem to get around. My buddies get away with murder, and I can't do anything without getting caught. Life sucks a big one.

Barry, 19, army

16. For married men: How long have you been married and do you have a good marriage?

I am proud to say that I have been married for twenty years. I believe that we have a strong and healthy marriage. I love my wife deeply and I am the only man she has known sexually.

Will, 47, jeweler

We have been married for three years. She slept with my brother two weeks ago. I threw her out. Technically I'm still married, but it doesn't matter anymore.

Wesley, 39, band director

Martha and I have been newlyweds for twenty-five years. I simply adore her and she makes me complete. For the life of me I couldn't imagine me without her.

Robert, 50, building contractor

17. Where do you place the credit for having a good marriage or relationship?

I have to place the credit with my wife. She has kept us together with her trust, love, and a lot of patience and understanding. She is truly heaven-sent.

Nicholas, 75, retired mechanic

I must give credit to both of us, my wife and myself. Our marriage is working because we both work hard at it. We communicate, we trust, we are understanding of each other's needs and supportive in every way. Our sex life hits the rafters and we aim to keep it there. I love her.

Scott, 45, automotive manufacturing manager

It's such a miracle, I'd have to give the credit to God. It's a wonder that woman can live with me. I can hardly tolerate myself.

B.J., 33, cellular phone salesman

18. If you have a troubled relationship with your mate, where do you place the blame?

When we hit rough spots, we talk it out to solve the issues at hand. We try not to blame each other. So far this approach has worked well.

Steve, 38, construction worker

I'm the bad seed in my marriage. I wasn't always that way, but somewhere in life's path I got tired of it all and sorta gave up. I need an overhaul. I wish I could go back to the carefree days when I had my youth—my wonderful attitude, and my libido was like the Eveready bunny.

Martino, 51, consultant

19. For those who are intentionally not married, why are you not married?

I'm not married because I choose not to be. I still have plenty of time for that. I am young and I have not found the one that I want to spend the rest of my life with.

Jobe, 24, phone operator

I hate the rules and regulations. I hate people, all people—any people—knowing where I am and why. My business is my business. I've always been this way. I'm a free spirit and don't wish to change.

Steve, 26, accountant

It's a prison, a place for rejects and retards. Life is too short. I'm too young and full of piss and vinegar to get tied down to a warden.

Todd, 30, computer programmer

20. What does commitment mean to you?

Doggie leash.

Trent, 19, student

I am terrified of commitment. I get all choked up when she starts talking commitment. I usually end the relationship at that point. I have not found the one that I am head over heels in love with. I am not going to rush into any long-term commitment.

Jose, 24, X-ray technician

According to Webster's, it means "the state of being obligated or emotionally impelled." I get emotional with women often, but compelled? No way. I'm compelled only to me and for me. I like my privacy and independence. Women seek and destroy those attributes like a torpedo on a mission.

Marcus, 24, drafting engineer

21. Is it easy for you to commit to a woman and your relationship with her?

Duh, its hard for any man to commit to anything, much less a relationship.

Andre, 29, bartender

It's not easy—no pain, no gain—but well worth it if you can do it. I had trouble with my first wife. I ran around, I drank, I didn't handle my business well and lost it all. When I decided to be in control of myself and my life, things started to change drastically for the better. Now in my second marriage I find life is very fulfilling. I eat right, sleep right, I'm happy and enjoying every minute of every day. I'm lucky to have had a second chance. Men should appreciate the goodness that stares them in the face and take nothing for granted. Sometimes we're just slow learners.

Mike, 49, lawyer

Nothing is easy with women. I don't understand what makes them tick. I only understand what ticks them off and gets them off.

Wesley, 25, truck driver

22. If you have trouble committing, why do you?

Why is the earth round? Why is the sky blue? Why do birds sing? If I knew the answer to any of these life questions, then maybe I would be richer and happy in a lasting relationship.

Stephen, 37, machinist

I am not ready to be roped.

Zach, 24, bouncer

You can't harness a wild stallion, and I don't want to be broken by any mare.

Buddy, 34, realtor

I like to give women pleasure. I'd like to find an older woman that's been sex starved for the last few years and change her oil about every hour on the hour.

Neal, 26, office supply manager

23. Why is it important to the majority of women to have a committed, monogamous relationship with a man?

It's instinct for a woman to settle down with one man and reproduce. They have a clock inside them and they need a mate for that. I am glad they are not like the black widow spiders because there are a lot of snakes like me out there in this cruel world.

Harry, 38, horse trainer

Women always know what is best. Father knows best is a crock.

Charles, 42, telemarketing supervisor

Seems to me women want to achieve the same goals men do. Fortune, power, sexual satisfaction, and success. I say suck, suck, until you succeed.

Warren, 44, office manager

24. How do you feel about domestic abuse?

They should take all the abusers and hang them up by their toes in a public square. Let the abused victim dole out the punishment.

Dustin, 24, rodeo clown

I think they should castrate all sex offenders. Beat every other day the ones that are physical. The ones that mentally abuse should be tortured to show them how it feels. I have no pity for the ones that abuse innocent people, no matter who they are.

Montel, 37, bookbinding company owner

I despise domestic abuse of any kind. The one who does this is not a man.

Owen, 48, doctor

Guys that participate in this sick activity should be shot, or better yet, castrated. What a jerk you'd have to be to beat up on women and children.

Craig, 36, hot-tub manufacturing

25. How do you feel about deadbeat dads?

They should be publicly humiliated like the kids are when they don't have the necessities of life. The dads that want to play instead of pay should be in jail. They were there to help produce the kids, they should be there to raise them.

Thirston, 40, telephone lineman

They should be beaten to death.

Lee, 48, teacher

Why is it there are so many good adults in the world that would give their right arm to have children and can't? And then there are parents that completely ignore their children and their responsibilities to them. Life is strange, but deadbeat dads are some of the lowest scum around.

Bruce, 31, reporter

26. Financial fears: If you have them, what are they and what do you believe causes them?

The pay does not stay caught up with the cost of living. It is commonly called inflation, smaller paychecks, and increased cost of products.

Toby, 23, unemployed

Four little words: our government at work.

Jeremy, 36, rights activist

Hell, yes, I've got financial fears—since the day Bill Clinton took office.

Gary, 52, entrepreneur

27. What personal achievement are you the most proud of?

That I have lived this long and not caught some killer disease.

Tim, 32, model

My children. I'm a great husband, but that's a much easier ambition and profession, if you will, than being a great father. The way schools are now, and life in general, being a good father is tough. I work hard, and still when I come home, I save time—make time for my children. They are life's reward. I love to watch their faces when I come through the door.

Alan, 45, computer programmer

I'm proud that I take good care of my family. I do things with my children, I truly love my wife. I'm proud that my teenagers haven't driven me completely to the nuthouse. I still have some sign of intelligence left and even have my sense of humor. Well, most of the time.

Gordon, 49, chemist

28. What would you like to accomplish that you haven't?

Personal wealth, happiness, and a woman that will love me for myself.

Paul, 26, ad salesman

Bliss with a woman. I am financially secure.

Toby, 46, bank vice president

I'd like to learn to fly through our friendly skies. To be up there next to the clouds and soar with the eagles makes my heart zing. I've learned how to do just about everything there is to do on the ground. Now I'm ready for the big bright blue yonder.

Owen, 47, rancher

29. What scares you?

Things that go bump in the night.

Terrance, 61, retired banker

Marriage. Love. Fatherhood. I'm forty-five and still feel like a scared small boy of thirteen. Women are much better at living fearlessly than men, by nature.

Hank, 45, restaurant equipment supply owner

Ugly women.

Peter, 24, student

30. Are you in touch with your so-called feminine side?

What you talking about? I have no so-called feminine side or any other female things. I am all man.

Ernest, 35, basketball coach

With a name like mine, I learned how to survive at an early age. So I don't have anything feminine except my name, and if you want to say something about that, then we can discuss it later.

Shannon, 31, boxer

My so-called feminine side is my butt. My baby loves my butt so much I formally gave it to her about four years ago. She tattooed her name right on that sucker. Couldn't you just see *that* in a divorce court?

Sidney, 30, gymnastics instructor

31. Do you express your fears, emotions, and desires openly with your mate?

My wife and I have an open and honest relationship. I am secure enough in myself that I can talk to her about my needs, desires, emotions, etc., and I have no fear about her holding it against me at a later time.

Keith, 35, sales associate

You must be kidding. She would never let me hear the end of it and I'm too afraid to try, even if I might be wrong. I wish I could. Sexually speaking, I always say what's on my mind, and seldom get what I want.

Lawrence, 36, stonemason

When I've had a tough day, or my sweetheart has had one, we climb into bed with a bowl of ice cream and two spoons. We talk about the day and eat our ice cream. It's been a sacred ritual since we first married twenty years ago. We never go to bed angry at each other, and we always have plenty of Ben & Jerry's in the freezer. Life is much better that way.

Lloyd, 57, law professor

32. What does being a man mean to you?

Having a dick in my pants and having to earn enough money to do the things I want to in life.

Joel, 38, computer programmer

I have a penis instead of a vagina.

Burt, 24, furniture salesman

Impeccable integrity. Always.

Howard, 44, insurance adjuster

30 Other Animals

1. ***How are you like an animal at times?***
2. ***What do you envy about an animal?***
3. ***What animalistic traits do you have, admire, or are reluctant to admit to?***
4. ***What real animal would you be if you could?***
5. ***What pet or childhood animal meant more to you than a girl, and why?***
6. ***What will a woman get from her dog that she won't get from you?***
7. ***Why do you think some women believe men are animals?***
8. ***Are you a womanizer? Or, have you ever been?***
9. ***Why are some women afraid of men?***
10. ***What is the meanest thing you ever did to a woman? What motivated you?***
11. ***What has a pet done for you that a woman hasn't?***

1. How are you like an animal at times?

When I am in my primal-man mode, I am a total animal with my baby. I take care of my most basic needs: the urge to survive and reproduce. I make love with energy, passion, almost violent emotions. I grunt and sweat and sometimes even squeal like a hog in heat. I thrust as hard and as deep as any animal in the jungle.

Manuel, 32, drywall installer

I'm like a pet dog in that I love my women unconditionally. They treat me like dirt, I wag my tail and lick their faces. They treat me mean, I bring them their slippers and watch over them at night. I'm faithful, obedient, and loyal. I'm the best pet a woman ever had.

Jack, 27, groundskeeper

I am like an animal only when in heat and looking for a piece of tail. Then I come on quick and stealthily like a cat looking for prey. The rest of the time I am just a teddy bear.

Ben, 36, bank associate

2. What do you envy about an animal?

The thing I envy is their ability to reproduce with one and go on with their life and not bother with that female again.

Jacob, 21, modeling student

I envy that their only worry is staying alive.

Patrick, 27, teacher

Absolutely nothing except having the ability and freedom to go to the bathroom anywhere, anytime. Sometimes I wish I could take a dump on my neighbor's front porch. That bastard pisses me off.

Taylor, 35, auto dealership owner

3. What animalistic traits do you have, admire, or are reluctant to admit to?

I'm not sure if this is what you are looking for, but when I take a dump, I always look in the bowl to see what I've done. At least I don't stick my nose in it like my poodle, Benny.

Allen, 25, research technician

I am a sex animal. I need to make love to survive, so I believe it must go back to my animal roots. I think my genes are affecting my need to drop my jeans as often as possible.

Troy, 22, security guard

My girlfriend says I am a dog, and sometimes I go out of my way to prove her right.

Brian, 20, student

I'm reluctant to admit that I do act like an animal at times. I have several animalistic traits, all of which require real talent, like taking a piss by a tree in the woods, eating with my bare hands—cramming it in as fast as I can go, as if I haven't eaten in a month. I growl like a bear when my wife tries to wake me from my "den." However, I really don't admire any of them. I'm just stuck with them and she's stuck with me. Love truly is blind as a bat.

Nathan, 32, graphic artist

4. What real animal would you be if you could?

I would be a lion, king of the jungle.

John, 29, electrician

I guess I would have to be an jackass, because I am an ass most of the time anyway.

Terrell, 28, musician

A pussycat. My wife likes the cat more than me. Sometimes I wonder if it's that scratchy little tongue he possesses. And I wonder what she lets him do with that scratchy thing.

Troy, 24, bridge builder

5. What pet or childhood animal meant more to you than a girl, and why?

When I was very small, I had a dog named Tinydog. Not "Tiny" or "dog" but "Tinydog." She was a dog-pound reject, but I loved her with all my heart. She would do anything for me. I rode her around the yard. I tied ribbons and tin cans to her ears. I fed her leftovers that made me want to puke. She even protected me from the neighborhood bullies. And yet she loved me totally and completely until the day she was hit by our next-door neighbor's car. She was running across the yards to come play with me, and she was smacked right in the head. She died in the driveway.

Pete, 28, computer programmer

I had a pet chicken that I literally ran to death when I was five. She was an Easter present that grew up, and she was always by my side. Looking back, I must have looked totally stupid running around the neighborhood with my Roy Rogers cowboy outfit and my pet chicken. But at the time I thought it was totally logical. She was my best friend. We had grand adventures in our backyard fort. I would ride my stick pony and chase

Polly all over the place. One day I was doing my regular routine chasing her around the garbage cans when she fell over and just plain died. I still don't know if chickens can have heart attacks, but I do know that I cried all night. Dad buried her next to my backyard fort, and I wouldn't go near it or her grave for the longest time.

Adam, 43, schoolteacher

During my childhood, I had a German shepherd that was my best friend. We grew up with each other. We went everywhere together. The dog even slept with me, and she didn't hog the bed either. She loved me unconditionally unlike the women of my older years have done. When my dog died of old age, I thought my world would end. I didn't sleep or eat for a week.

Stephen, 36, plumber

I always liked my dog Rex because he would lick my dick anytime I wanted it. If I could get that same kind of response from my wife, I might like her more.

Mac, 25, machinist

6. What will a woman get from her dog that she won't get from you?

Nothing. If I love a woman, I love her totally. I am her love slave, I will do anything for her.

Jerry, 28, public transportation

She won't get the obedience from me that she gets from that poor old scared dog of hers.

Charlie, 67, taxidermist

7. Why do you think some women believe men are animals?

Some men simply are animals to women. I hear guys talking trash at work, and they brag about the crummy things they do to their girlfriends. I wouldn't put up with it if I were a woman, so why should they? I think a lot of men deserve their bad reputations. Maybe if their women would give them a little of their own medicine, they'd straighten up.

Maurice, 31, gym instructor

I know women think men are animals because most men keep putting their noses into places they shouldn't be, always sniffing and smelling. It is embarrassing, especially when the guy is old enough to know better.

Max, 45, retailer

So far throughout history men have proved women right in thinking that they are animals. Maybe someday the men will stop acting their IQ and start acting their age.

Damien, 45 truck driver

Uhhh, because they are?

Ron, 28, tire manufacturer

8. Are you a womanizer? Or, have you ever been?

In my younger years, I tried to sow every oat I came across. Maybe I was afraid they would all rot if I didn't get to them in time. Now I am happy just to be able sow one oat.

Jeb, 58, semiretired

I'm the best at it, the most ashamed of it, and wish I could stop. I've been this way for as long as I can remember, and women even expect it from me. It's like they take one look at me and know that's what I do best. I even announce it, as if that will cover the sins of it. The part I can't figure is why they still want me. I am good in the sack, in fact I'm real good, but I'm emotionally impotent.

Joe, 45, doctor

9. Why are some women afraid of men?

Men are bigger, stronger, and, I believe, meaner. They talk about how a scorned woman is something to watch out for, but you should see a 250-pound, jealous, insecure drunk on a rampage. A little 100-pound secretary doesn't stand a chance unless she has a 350 magnum under her pillow.

Rob, 31, pool maintenance supervisor

Women are afraid to trust men or love them because they will be betrayed. It isn't a question of if they will be betrayed, but only when it will happen. After you have been burned a dozen times, you learn to hold back your feelings, trust, and love.

Barry, 36, interior decorator

Some women have never had a successful relationship with men in their entire life, so naturally they are afraid, doubtful, and insecure. One bad apple spoils the barrel, and when it comes to men, I'm sure you can go through a dozen barrels without finding one decent specimen. It's a wonder more women aren't gay.

Kevin, 50, taxi driver

Today's law, that's the reason. They let men abuse women, then just slap the men's hand and tell them don't do that again. I feel we should do more to stop the abuse than the past generations. We should show them that not all men are alike.

Frank, 43, carpenter

Because they've earned it. Men can be total assholes. That's one of the reasons I had my sex-change operation. I couldn't tolerate the guilt by association to the male gender.

Patrice, 28, dancer

10. What is the meanest thing you ever did to a woman? What motivated you?

Maybe this qualifies, but as a young boy, I put a frog down Melissa's dress one day. I thought it would be a cool joke in front of the other kids. Unknown to me she was scared of frogs, and the look of terror on her face quickly took the prank and put it in its place. I felt so bad I tried to make it up to her every day. To make this story short, she ended up falling in love with me, so I guess the joke was on me. In fact we got married and have two wonderful kids ourselves.

Bart, 49, certified public accountant

I loved her deeply and left. I broke her heart. I was motivated by selfishness, insecurity, and fear of failure. I made her suffer needlessly, and I feel sad and ashamed.

Mike, 45, electrician

11. What has a pet done for you that a woman hasn't?

I have yet to find a woman who will bring me my slippers.

Horace, 45, outdoorsman

My cat, Snowball, will lick the head of my penis if I haven't taken a shower in a couple of days.

Sid, 24, musician

My poodle humped my leg in the middle of a shopping spree downtown, and my wife has never even come close to that kind of public display of affection.

Burt, 35, marketing specialist

A pet gives unconditional love expecting nothing in return but food, water, and maybe a pat on the head. I wish woman were so easy to please.

Jared, 28, sales

Obey me. Talk to me. Go fishing with me. Hell, I can't get my girlfriend to cook my breakfast without practically burning the kitchen down, and you know what they say . . . it only takes three minutes to burn an entire trailer house completely to the ground.

Chuck, 36, painter

And Finally . . .

You've survived. Congratulations. We hope you had fun and learned a few things, maybe even a new trick or technique you can show your lovers. If you have more questions now than you did when you started, we have accomplished our goal.

We love fan mail, comments, observations, and plain old chit-chat. If you have any desire to communicate, you can reach us in care of:

THE GOOD GIRLS
P.O. Box 50214
Belle Meade Station
Nashville, TN 37205

If you enjoyed the men's comments, you might also enjoy reading the female point of view. Our first book, *The Good Girls' Guide to Great Sex* [Three Rivers Press, 0-609-80176-7, $12.00 ($16.00 in Canada)], is available at fine bookstores everywhere. More than 5,000 women of all ages, backgrounds, and experiences shared their most intimate thoughts on sex, men, and relationships. You will be amazed at their candid comments.

Thanks for your support. Be careful. Be sweet.

About the Authors

Thom W. King is an award-winning fashion photographer. He has also worked as a photojournalist and reporter. His passions are collecting bad art and driving convertibles.

Debora Peterson is an accomplished singer/songwriter. She has extensive media experience, including radio and television. She was born in France, grew up in Montana, and now lives in Tennessee.